THE MODERN ARABIC LITERARY LANGUAGE

Georgetown University Classics in Arabic Language and Linguistics
Karin C. Ryding and Margaret Nydell, series editors

This series makes available seminal publications in Arabic language and linguistics which have gone out of print. Chosen for their quality of research and scholarship, these books will serve the growing national and international need for reference works on Arabic language and culture, as well as provide access to quality textbooks and audiovisual resources for teaching Arabic language in its written and spoken forms.

Arabic Language Handbook
Mary Catherine Bateson

The Arabic Language Today
A. F. L. Beeston

The Arabic Linguistic Tradition
Georges Bohas, Jean-Patrick Guillaume, and Djamel Kouloughli

A Basic Course in Iraqi Arabic with MP3 Audio Files
Wallace M. Erwin

A Basic Course in Moroccan Arabic with MP3 Files
Richard S. Harrell with Mohammed Abu-Talib and William S. Carroll

A Dictionary of Iraqi Arabic: English—Arabic, Arabic—English
English—Arabic edited by B. E. Clarity, Karl Stowasser, Ronald G. Wolfe
Arabic—English edited by D. R. Woodhead and Wayne Beene

A Dictionary of Moroccan Arabic: Moroccan–English/English–Moroccan
Richard S. Harrell and Harvey Sobelman, Editors

A Dictionary of Syrian Arabic: English—Arabic
Karl Stowasser and Moukhtar Ani, Editors

Eastern Arabic with MP3 Files
Frank A. Rice and Majed F. Sa'id

Formal Spoken Arabic Basic Course with MP3 Files, Second Edition
Karin C. Ryding and David Mehall

Formal Spoken Arabic FAST Course with MP3 Files
Karin C. Ryding and Abdelnour Zaiback

Modern Arabic: Structures, Functions, and Varieties, Revised Edition
Clive Holes

The Modern Arabic Literary Language: Lexical and Stylistic Developments
Jaroslav Stetkevych

A Reference Grammar of Syrian Arabic with Audio CD
Mark W. Cowell

A Short Reference Grammar of Iraqi Arabic
Wallace M. Erwin

A Short Reference Grammar of Moroccan Arabic with Audio CD
Richard S. Harrell

THE MODERN ARABIC LITERARY LANGUAGE

Lexical and Stylistic Developments

Jaroslav Stetkevych

Georgetown University Press
Washington D.C.

To William R. Polk,
a rare man, a friend

Наша ціль—людське щастя і воля,
Розум владний без віри основ,
І братерство велике, всесвітнє . . .

Ivan Franko

As of January 1, 2007, 13-digit ISBN numbers will replace the current 10-digit system.
Paperback: 978-1-58901-117-5

Georgetown University Press, Washington, D.C.

Library of Congress Cataloging-in-Publication Data

Stetkevych, Jaroslav.
The modern Arabic literary language : lexical and stylistic developments / Jaroslav Stetkevych.
p. cm. — (Georgetown classics in Arabic language and linguistics)
Originally published: Chicago : University of Chicago Press, 1970. (Publications of the Center for Middle Eastern Studies ; no. 6)
Includes bibliographical references and index.
ISBN 1-58901-117-1 (alk. paper)
1. Arabic language—History. I. Title. II. Series. III. Series: Publications of the Center for Middle Eastern Studies ; no. 6.
PJ6075.S7 2006
492.709—dc22

2006040919

This book is printed on acid-free paper meeting the requirements of the American National Standard for Permanence in Paper for Printed Library Materials.

13 12 11 10 09 08 07 06 9 8 7 6 5 4 3 2
First printing

Printed in the United States of America

Contents

Foreword to the Georgetown Classics Edition

I count it a great privilege to be able to write an introduction to the reprinted text of Jaroslav Stetkevych's path-breaking work on the development of a modern Arabic literary language, a work that is now some thirty-six years old. Such is my respect for him as a scholar and colleague that I did not pause before accepting the offer. However, as I have contemplated the process of writing these lines, the daunting nature of what I have agreed to do has come home to roost. While I may have remembered the contents of the book and the significant role that they have played in our developing understanding of language-change within the Arabic-speaking world, I had forgotten that the original publication carried a foreword by none other than Sir Hamilton Gibb, professor of Arabic at Oxford and later at Harvard, and the undisputed doyen of Anglophone Arabic studies during the first half of the twentieth century. It was while Gibb was at Harvard that Jaroslav Stetkevych came there to obtain a second doctorate under the great scholar's direction (having obtained his first doctoral degree in Spain). The obvious respect that Gibb had for his already-accomplished student is reflected not merely in the foreword to the first edition but also in an interesting anecdote contained in the introduction to a recent translation of Andalusian narrative undertaken by another Harvard student of those days, James

Monroe, now of Berkeley. Monroe tells us how Gibb asked Stetkevych to give the younger student a hand in coping with the complexities of the Arabic texts that were being read in Gibb's seminars.

In such terms I too can count myself as a student of Jaroslav Stetkevych. In 1966, Stetkevych, now an assistant professor at the University of Chicago, had a sabbatical year that was spent—as have been many others since—in Cairo (during the course of which he was, I presume, working on the completion of this particular volume). That happened to be the year in which I was in Cairo, conducting my own research for the doctoral degree at Oxford, I being the first student from that institution to focus research on the modern period (a direct consequence of the arrival of M. M. Badawi at the university as lecturer in modern Arabic literature in 1963). I was one of a group of students (another was Michael Zwettler, now at the Ohio State University, and still another, J. Dennis Hyde, now retired from his post at the University of Pennsylvania Library) who, during the course of that year (culminating in the June War of 1967), benefited greatly from lengthy conversations with Professor Stetkevych, whose erudition and his willingness to share it with us "novices" were a model for emulation.

It was, of course, Gibb himself who had served in a pioneer role in anglophone scholarship on modern Arabic literature, having published a series of articles on the subject in the *Bulletin of the School of Oriental and African Studies* (beginning in 1928) that were later published in a collection of his articles edited by Stanford Shaw and William Polk (*Studies on the Civilization of Islam*, London: Routledge & Kegan Paul, 1962). By the year 1970, when Stetkevych's work was first published, the study of modern Arabic had advanced and improved somewhat. In the 1940s Denys Johnson-Davies and Aubrey (Abba) Eban had published pioneering translations of fictional works; and Pierre Cachia had published (1947) the first study of a modern Arab littérateur (Taha Husayn). The 1950s saw the post-Sputnik promulgation in the United States of the National Defense and Education Act (NDEA, 1957), with its focus on the study of modern languages and area studies, and its analogue in Britain, the Hayter Report of the early 1960s.

By 1966 the Middle East Studies Association had been created as a means of fostering and promoting this rapidly expanding interest in the regions of Northern Africa and Western Asia, along with increased focus on the learning of their languages. This is the context into which the initial publication of Stetkevych's work was inserted. Like another hugely important study of the period, Albert Hourani's *Arabic Thought in the Liberal Age* (1962), it focused on developments in the nineteenth century and into the twentieth as being a crucial element in any assessment of the course of events and cultural trends in the years following the independence of Arab nations in the 1950s and beyond. *The Modern Arabic Literary Language* is thus one of those foundational studies upon which a great deal of subsequent research has been based. Parenthetically, I might point out that some of those much needed disciplinary foundations are still in process: The first decade of the twenty-first century, for example, has witnessed the publication of the first two linguistically based studies of the modern Arabic language (Badawi, Carter, and Gully [2005]; Ryding [2005]), that being the very topic whose development is explored in this newly published edition of Stetkevych's work.

The Modern Arabic Literary Language studies, as its subtitle indicates, "lexical and stylistic developments." The author's purpose, as stated in his preface, is "to present a methodical review of the processes that led to the modernization of the Arabic language." I would like here to focus on two of the words he uses: "developments" and "methodical." The word "developments" implies a process and sequence, and the great benefit that Stetkevych brings to this study is his enormous knowledge of and acquaintance with the classical tradition of the Arabic language and the critical scholarship on that tradition (applying in particular to the analogical processes involved in the Arabic lexicographical system based on verbal roots and the methods of "*ishtiqaq*" [derivation]). This work may have taken developments from the nineteenth century onward as its major focus, but it is firmly grounded in the pre-modern tradition of Arabic language-analysis.

The second term, "methodical," could well be characterized as a substantial understatement. Gibb points out that this study took ten years to complete, and that is in no small part because Stetkevych set himself to study the phenomenon of language-change through as many of the source texts as possible, combing his way through the reports, publications, and even the minutes of the Arabic Language Academy as it wrestled with the issues of language-transformation and neologisms. Gibb characterizes the results of such a huge project as "a terse and original essay," but at this point it is important to note that, as is the case with all of Stetkevych's works, the text that is presented to us constitutes the distillation of a colossal amount of reading and research, information and opinion that has been processed and filtered through a critical mind of the highest order.

So thirty-six years after its initial appearance, Georgetown University Press makes available once again one of the classic twentieth century studies of modern Arabic, penned by one of its greatest scholars. Such is its enduring value that a new generation of Arabists will continue to benefit from its availability.

Roger Allen

Foreword

It is a century or so since writers in Arabic found themselves faced with difficulties in utilizing Western terms dealing with modern subjects. Many of them sought means of expressing scientific and other technical terms in various ways, most of which fell by the wayside. Almost forty years ago the Arabic Academy was charged with the task of remodelling the ancient linguistic structure to fit modern use. By then, however, many of the terms were already too well established to be altered; nevertheless, there were still some tens of thousands of words for which no Arabic term was found adequate, and both Academicians and non-Academicians have steadily reduced the number of these words.

Today the Arabic reader can find expressions in his own language with most of which he is well satisfied. How this modern structure has been expanding words and meanings, by assimilating new sources or by other measures, is a study in itself, and Professor Stetkevych has put all Arabists in his debt by defining what has been done and is being done to develop the modern Arabic style. He has devoted ten years to this study and has summed up the results of his investigation in a terse and original essay. What he has given us is the first examination of this newest development by showing it in its context as Arabic, through reference to its illustration in daily usage. It is a very impressive achievement and one that is most striking; it shows that in most respects the language is closer today to the language of al-Jāḥiẓ than it was one hundred years ago.

Sir Hamilton Gibb

Introduction

As an historian, concerned with the development of the modern Middle East, I take a selfish view of Professor Stetkevych's work. I shall not, therefore, emphasize in this introduction what its obvious merits are as a work of scholarship on the development of the modern Arabic literary language. Rather, I propose to dwell on what I believe to be an even more important though indirect product of his scholarship. What I suggest that Professor Stetkevych has given us is a sharper tool of analysis and a larger body of materials for the cultural history of the modern Middle East than we have had before.

Both the context and the issue of this book can be set forth in a few highly foreshortened notes on Arabic-Islamic history.

The Arabs, although heirs to a proud and coherent civilization which had reached its peak at the time of the European Dark Ages, with an empire stretching from France to China, were exhausted by the enormity of the task they had undertaken and depleted by the physical dispersion of their resources. Consequently, coming under the domination of fellow Muslim Turks, Mongols, Berbers, and Persians, the Arabs fell into a long "sleep," from the end of the thirteenth until the nineteenth century. During this period they did not participate significantly in the cultural, economic, or political life of the world or even of the Middle East. They engaged in no further conquests and ceased even to govern themselves. At least in the Mediterranean, the Arabs were no longer the great merchants. Their scholars lapsed into a habit of merely repeating past learning, and even in this habit they became so lethargic that not only was the creative impulse lost but the conservation of Arabic learning was jeopardized.

From this sleep they were rudely aroused by the Napoleonic expedition to Egypt in 1798. Overwhelmed, first militarily and then in a variety of other and ever more subtle ways throughout the nineteenth century, they abandoned their older forms of life under the "impact" of the West. By the end of the nineteenth century, so alarmed were many of the Arab leaders at what appeared to be deculturalization that they undertook a struggle to recapture a sense of identity. It is with one aspect of this struggle that Professor Stetkevych deals.

Such, in only slightly caricatured form, is the conventional view of Arabic history held until quite recently in the West and in the Middle East as well. While recent research has tended to modify a number of aspects of this view, it will serve our purpose here in two ways. Even in this abbreviated form, it gives us a starting point for the analysis of the main problem in the history of the period that concerns Professor Stetkevych.

More important, as a view accepted in the Middle East itself, it was an integral ingredient in the intellectual conflict of that period. The Arabic thinkers with whom Professor Stetkevych deals accepted as correct the historical sequence of the Golden Age, the "long sleep," and the "awakening." They believed that the period in Arabic history that, chronologically, corresponded to the Renaissance, the Reformation, and the Enlightenment in Europe was functionally comparable with the European Dark Ages. That is to say, it was a sort of curtain pulled down between Arabs of the nineteenth century and the great days of their past. But it is important to stress that the "great days of their past" were not just, as in the West, the flowering of a vaguely related culture—in the way that Greece and Rome were vaguely related to Britain and France—but were directly related to the men of this period linguistically, religiously, and, as the Arabs loved to emphasize, by ties of kinship.

The concept of kinship need not detain us except in one regard. With identity and identification such evocative words in Western civilization, it is worth noting that the Arabs—however diverse they may have been in terms of actual ancestry—identified closely and directly with the great figures of the Golden Age. There was, consequently, along with each of their attempts at modernization, a lengthy look over their shoulder toward the past. This was to prove both constructive and inhibiting. Constructively, the Arabic speakers of the nineteenth century were assured that they *could* aspire to a position of significance in the world, since those with whom they were associated had, in past times, played a comparable role. This immediately set them off from most of their African neighbors, who had no such sense of historical accomplishment. It gave them a certain pride and sense of confidence. However, this preoccupation with the past was so intense as to inhibit creativity. Further, the very coherence of Arabic-Islamic civilization served as a protective layer, inhibiting the introduction of what were regarded, even by Middle Easterners, as important aspects of reform and modernization. The utilization of such apparently "value-free" tools as the telegraph occasioned great soul-searching by those who were concerned with the preservation of culture. When the tools, the goods, and the mores of Western society entered the Middle East, they did so unsanctioned, and severe conflicts arose between those ready to accept them and those violently opposed to them.

As for the other two major ties to the Golden Age—language and religion—we must understand the ways in which they interplayed to form a duality of cultural impulse. This is obviously a subject of vast dimensions, but here a few notes will suffice to stress the value of Professor Stetkevych's study.

Throughout most of the history of the Middle East, Arabic was the medium in which the message of Islam was embodied and through which it was transmitted from generation to generation. As the Koran stresses, Islam is a religion brought to the Arabs in their language, as previous peoples had received their messages from God in their languages. Through all the vicissitudes of Arabic history, the study of language formed an extremely important part of the curriculum of schools of theology. A full and correct interpretation of the Koran was essential to the religious base of the culture. Such minor aspects of the language as calligraphy came to have an artistic importance, and an intimate knowledge of such subjects as syntax and grammar were not only in the abstract the mark of an educated man but formed the materials of the intricate literary games in which the Arabs delight. Finally, religion was as much the conveyor of the language as the language was the conveyor of religion. As the Arabs and others spread Islam, it became necessary for the new Muslims to learn the language of the Koran.

But there were periods in the history of the Middle East when the language and the religion were not so interpenetrated. The most obvious is the century before the advent of Islam. This is the period that has given to Arabic-Islamic civilization its classical literature, which, although the result of pagan cultures and expressing a social ethos often in conflict with Islam, is so highly prized as the linguistic treasury of Arabic as to be brought into the schools of theology.

Toward the end of the nineteenth century, as materials for the literary revival came to be assembled, those concerned with this task were often, particularly in the Levant, non-Muslims. Even if such men were not Christian, as some of the more famous in the Levant were, they were at some pains to distinguish themselves from fellow-Muslim theologians whose obscurantism made them ideologically unacceptable to the modernizers. Since Islam was not a politically acceptable mode of identification, these men sought a unifying principle in their Arabic heritage.

Indeed, we may for purposes of analysis, at least, distinguish between the Islamic modernizers—Jamal ad-Din al-Afghani, Muhammad Abdu, and others—who sought in a revived Islamic religion their principal means of defense against incursions from the West and against loss of cultural identity and those who, like the subjects of this book, sought in the Arabic language a similar means of defense and sense of identity.

Perhaps a closer look at what was happening in the Middle East in the nineteenth century will help to clarify the political and cultural challenges for which religious and linguistic answers were sought.

Relatively speaking—that is, relative to Europe in the contemporary period and to Islamic society at an earlier period—the Arabic speakers of the Middle East in the nineteenth century *were* backward. They lacked the techniques and the tools of organized society. In many categories of the economic and social life of the average citizen, the disparity between the Arabic parts of the Middle East and Europe was smaller than between the developed and underdeveloped parts of the world today. In the capacity to create and organize human skills—the capacity we are learning increasingly to appreciate in judging the contrast between the developed and underdeveloped countries of our time—the Middle East was much poorer than Europe. Men in that period were aware of the reality of, but did not agree on the reasons for, disparity of power.

In a sense, the history of the nineteenth century may be viewed as a deepening understanding of the reasons for the repeated failure of Middle Easterners to stand up against Western power. At first, the "answer" was sought in trivial external appearances: Middle Eastern soldiers were dressed up to look like European soldiers. As understanding increased, the soldiers were armed with similar equipment and trained in similar tactics. Yet, as we so clearly understand today, this superficial reordering did not alter the intrinsic imbalances of power. Reformers of all kinds probed into the problem. Schools were opened and factories built, land reclaimed from the desert, dams constructed, ports opened, diseases stamped out, dress altered, new equipment introduced, laws enacted, study missions undertaken, institutions created, all in the vain hope that each new reform would bring with it a satisfying answer to the obvious weakness of the East.

While each reform was, in and of itself, on balance, of some value, the whole seldom was the equal of its parts. Rather, it was less. There remained, consequently, the nagging belief that some intrinsic, inner thing was still lacking. What was the "spirit" or "inner value" of the culture? Was not that, after all, both what was to be defended against the Europeans and what alone made a successful defense possible?

For most of the nineteenth century and in the minds of most of the people, this "spirit" was not "the nation." It was, instead, some largely undefinable or, perhaps more accurately, variously defined, conception of a way of life. As seen from the outside, this sense of difference from others expressed itself simply in xenophobia. The real quality of this feeling obviously differed among classes and groups of the society. The minorities and the upper class were much more open to Western influences than the lower and Muslim classes. Within each class or group certain categories of thought and action were more sacrosanct than others. Issues of religion were more impervious to outside influence than were those of technology; family life was more protected from changes of mores than was male organization; and, linguistically speaking, the cultural core, as expressed in the "classical" language, was more treasured and guarded by Arabic speakers than was the vernacular.

Along with a growing receptivity toward the Western intrusion came a growing self-consciousness about certain aspects of Middle Eastern identity.

Briefly, and at the risk of excessive distortion through oversimplification, it may be said that the quest for identity took two separate but overlapping forms. On the one hand, the reaction was in terms of religion. Throughout the nineteenth century, the society of the predominant population of Egypt continued to define itself chiefly in religious terms. As intellectual life quickened, in part because of the stimulus of the West, there was a renewed interest in Islam itself and a consequent attempt to strip away the later medieval accretions of Islamic society to get at the sources. In large part, this was an attempt to recapture the vigor and sureness of early Islam. The relative backwardness of contemporary Middle Eastern society was equated with the long "sleep" of the later Middle Ages, in which it was assumed (as we now know, erroneously) that the religious life had ceased to offer an intellectual stimulus.

On the other hand, speakers of Arabic, Christian and Muslim alike, sought to recover the sources of their *supra*-religious culture. The speakers of Arabic found language, even more than the Islamic religion, on which they disagreed, to be the core of their culture. The centrality of language, the fascination with the word, the concern with the medium rather than the message has long been remarked upon as a distinctive Semitic characteristic. Language is not *an* art form, it is *the* art of the Arabs. The threat of its obsolescence, corruption, or even loss was profoundly disquieting.

Far more than the speakers of French, Spanish, Russian, or other national-cultural-political languages, Arabic speakers sought to tighten the bonds of their language and to identify means of preserving its classical form, as well as its utility, in the modern world.

Two courses of action appeared possible. The first was to reassert the uniqueness, unity, and perfection of the language. While antiquarian in form, this movement represented a considerable gain over the torpid, imitative, and lazy approach to language of recent centuries. To those concerned with a reaction to Western penetration, the Arabic "purist" revival appeared a very attractive option.

Conversely, the introduction of Western individuals, forms, mores, goods, and services seemed to demand a wholly different linguistic thrust. Vulgarly, language became bifurcated. The literary language, restricted to the classical subjects, was treasured by all the educated groups, while the uneducated, those with educations oriented toward the West, and the general public moved practically and unsystematically toward the development of linguistic forms more suited to their current needs.

Reconciliation of these two divergent trends—both linguistically and philosophically—lies at the heart of the problem of modern Arabic linguistics.

It is easy for speakers of English, secure in the imperialism or even colonialism of their language—conquering and settling, as it were, whole vocabularies of German, French, Latin, and even Arabic—to scorn what appear to be puerile or at least pedantic defensive linguistics. Secure in the far-flung domain of our language, we cannot really understand the desperate defensiveness of those who stand against us. Is not language, after all, merely a means of communication, and, as such, to be judged solely in these pragmatic terms? If a better means is available, should it not be adopted? Can there be any real virtue in maintaining inefficient, obsolescent, or even obsolete languages? Surely serious men of affairs have more important tasks than to worry about the origins of words, their esoteric meanings, their linguistic "purity."

To the defenders of other languages, the case appears quite differently. Not alone the Arabs but the speakers of dozens of other languages have found in those languages not merely a means of communication but the genius of their nationhood. And not alone among the non-European languages has this been the case. We have only to remember the enormous influence of the Brothers Grimm upon the rise of German nationalism or the flowering of Russian literature in the mid-nineteenth century to appreciate this.

In short, without meaning to distort the purpose of Professor Stetkevych, who is concerned essentially with the language as a language—of which he has attained a mastery rare among Arabic scholars anywhere—I have attempted to set out here what I believe to be the broader historical, political, and cultural aspects of this study. In its own terms, it is an impressive work of scholarship. In the broader terms of modern cultural history, it enables us to see more deeply than before into the extraordinarily complex patterns of cultural conflict, regeneration, and symbiosis in the Middle East.

WILLIAM R. POLK

Preface

THIS book is an attempt to present a methodical review of the processes that led to modernization of the Arabic literary language. As such, the book is also an account of Arabic philological and linguistic efforts to meet the challenge of modernization. The extent and ramification of these efforts are reflected in the proportions of the individual chapters.

Thus most attention has been given to the application of the analogical method of derivation (chapter 1), since this constitutes the chief means of lexical enrichment within the rigorous framework of classical Arabic morphology. Chapters 2 and 3, on the compounding and use of foreign words, also reflect the theoretical preoccupations of Arabic linguistics with lexical matters. The problem of semantic extension (chapter 4) appears to me of equal importance with that of analogical derivation, even though thus far the former has received but little attention. The theoretical positions behind the question of simplification of Arabic grammar (chapter 5) chiefly reflect new attitudes rather than practical achievements. Chapter 6, relating semantic extension and simplification of the grammar, samples representative stylistic developments.

For valuable criticism of the manuscript, I wish to express my gratitude to Professor W. F. Wilferd Madelung.

JAROSLAV STETKEVYCH

The Analogical Method of Derivation (*Al-Qiyās*)

1

WHETHER Arabic possesses all those merits which are being so bountifully bestowed upon it by its zealous defenders is a matter of personal bias and, to a certain degree, even an academic topic. What remains certain is that, in a way, it is a privileged language. It has lived for one millennium and a half essentially unchanged, usually gaining, never completely losing. Venus-like, it was born in a perfect state of beauty, and it has preserved that beauty in spite of all the hazards of history and all the corrosive forces of time. It is true that there was not always that Praxitelean limpidity of line about it. Figuratively speaking, it has known its Gothic, its Renaissance and its Baroque periods. It has known austerity, holy ecstasy and voluptuousness, bloom and decadence. It exuberated in times of splendor and persisted through times of adversity in a state of near-hibernation. But when it awoke again, it was the same language. The fact that Arabic long survived and still had the vitality to burgeon anew might be due to religious and social factors, but the quantitative ability to expand and the qualitative capacity to attain perfection and to maintain its essential characteristics are merits of the language exclusively. Here we shall study these two aspects of Arabic: its physical growth and its apparent immutability. These aspects bear profoundly upon the very nature of the language and upon its present possibilities and future hopes.

To the Western student unfamiliar with the schematic morphological structure of Semitic languages, the first experience with Arabic suggests an idea of almost mathematical abstraction. The perfect system of the three radical consonants, the derived verbal forms with their basic meanings, the precise formation of the verbal noun, of the participles—everything is clarity, logic, system, and abstraction. The language is like a mathematical formula. This is, of course, a first notion but it also is the ultimate truth. In between there lies the great body of the language: rich and various, with its pitfalls and puzzles, but what impresses itself upon the mind is the abstract idea.

In the first Islamic century this abstract idea of the language began to take shape in the minds of men like ᵓAbū al-ᵓAswad al-Duᵓalī (died A.H. 67), and the science of Arabic grammar was born.[1] At first it was a purely empirical science. One observation led to another, thus revealing common characteristics and suggesting common rules. These first rules were, consequently, the product of similarity or analogy. Although analogy had not yet acquired its independent form of existence as criterion, its validity had begun to gain emphasis.[2] This was as yet an empirical result only. But after the empirical attitude had made sufficient headway—among the grammarians of Basra chiefly—so as to allow a deeper insight into the motives of the lan-

1. Henri Fleisch rejects the role of al-Duᵓalī as the originator of Arabic grammar. Instead, he proposes to start Arabic grammar one generation after al-Duᵓalī, with ᶜAbd al-Lāh Ibn ᵓAbī ᵓIsḥāq (died A.H. 117), who is the earliest source of Sībawayh. See *Traité de philologie arabe* (Beirut, 1961), 1:26–27.

2. *Qiyās* as a linguistic concept and as method germinated and defined itself in the relatively short span of time between ᶜAbd al-Lāh Ibn ᵓAbī ᵓIsḥāq (died A.H. 117) and al-Khalīl Ibn ᵓAḥmad (died A.H. 175). The latter, according to al-Sīrāfī, had already reached the utmost in establishing the validity of *qiyās*. See Fleisch, *Traité*, 1:27, 28 (footnotes). Without denying the importance of al-Khalīl, al-Sīrāfī's statement has to be treated as less absolute in the light of later development of *qiyās*.

guage, analogy itself was turned into a binding rule, powerful enough not only to explain, but also to correct and to form. Since then, analogy (*al-qiyās*), or the analogical method, has played a major role in the configuration of the Arabic language. It became the principal characteristic of the Basra school of grammarians. It also provided the essential distinction between the two rival schools of Basra and Kufa, and flourished in the later school of Baghdad, achieving its highest expression in the works of ᵓAbū ᶜAlī al-Fārisī (died A.H. 377) and his disciple, ᶜUthmān Ibn Jinnī (died A.H. 392). The *qiyās* is probably playing its most important role, however, during the philological revival that is taking place in our own days.

How did it happen that the principle of analogy became so powerful and vital a force in the Arabic language? Is it a criterion originally Arabic, or did it penetrate into Arabic scientific and intellectual life together with sciences and methodologies adopted from the Greeks?

Greek influence in Arabic philology is extremely difficult to trace. The beginnings of Arabic grammar reveal absolutely no such influence. As far as terminology and morphological and syntactic structuring are concerned, these can be considered parts of a properly Arabic science. A possibility of an indirect Greek influence upon the school of Basra, and particularly upon its later components, could be seen in the evidence of the analogical method so characteristically employed by them.[3] Otherwise, at least in the formative stages of Arabic grammar, we must not look for direct Greek traces. Furthermore, even in later stages, the evidence remains indirect only. Nevertheless, in dealing with other sciences and disciplines undoubtedly assimilated from the Greeks, we get the same picture of a striking lack of foreign-sounding terms which would hint at their source. In philosophy, and particularly in logic, the terminology is

3. Another philological conceptualization within the school of Basra —that of al-Zajjājī—concerning the precedence of the temporally indefinite *maṣdar* over the temporally defined verb may also be due to Greek influence. See the discussion of this problem by Mahdī al-Makhzūmī in his interesting book, *Fī al-Naḥw al-ᶜArabī: Naqd wa Tawjīh* (Sidon-Beirut, 1964), pp. 103–5, 144–45.

unmistakably Arabic, even though the disciplines are "assimilated sciences" (*ᶜulūm dakhīlah*). Moreover, when Hellenic sciences were introduced into Arabic in the early Abbasid time, Arabic language and grammar were in a certain stage of development already, and the vital principle of *qiyās* which made possible derivation (*ishtiqāq*) and creation of compound forms (*naḥt*), as well as arabization according to the spirit of the Arabic language (*taᶜrīb*), was already in force, permitting an effective creation of terminology capable of assimilating the *ᶜulūm dakhīlah*.

The Egyptian ᵓAḥmad ᵓAmīn suggests a different explanation of the *qiyās* in philology. According to him, philologists who recognize the principle of *qiyās*, like ᵓAbū ᶜAlī al-Fārisī and his disciple Ibn Jinnī, take a position in respect to the language which is analogous to that taken by ᵓAbū Ḥanīfah (died A.H. 150) in respect to jurisprudence (*fiqh*).[4] Furthermore, those two most outstanding representatives of *qiyās* were actually related to the school of ᵓAbū Ḥanīfah through the works of Muḥammad Ibn al-Ḥasan al-Shaybānī (died A.H. 189),[5] although they also were suspected of belonging to the *Muᶜtazilah*,[6] with its rational inquisitiveness. Particularly important is the role of ᶜUthmān Ibn Jinnī in the final formulation of the criterion of analogy.[7] His book *Al-Khaṣāᵓiṣ* contains three chapters related to the *qiyās*, besides frequent scattered allusions.[8] He tries to establish his principle as a science, as

4. ᵓAḥmad ᵓAmīn: *Ẓuhr al-ᵓIslām*, 2d ed. (Cairo, 1957), 2:89–92. Even though ᵓAḥmad ᵓAmīn is basically correct in establishing a connection between the use of the analogical method in jurisprudence and philology, this similarity of method is helpful only insofar as the later development of philological *qiyās* is concerned. The origins of the method remain obscure. The chronological evidence alone would indicate that *qiyās* was employed by Arab philologists at least one generation before it appeared in jurisprudence. Almost simultaneously with the work of ᵓAbū Ḥanīfah, *qiyās* was approaching its broad implementation by al-Khalīl Ibn ᵓAḥmad.

5. Muḥammad Ibn al-Najjār, in the introduction to his edition of Ibn Jinnī's *Al-Khaṣāᵓiṣ* (Cairo, 1952), 1:40–41.

6. Ibid., p. 42.

7. ᵓAbū ᶜAbd al-Lāh Yāqūt, *Muᶜjam al-ᵓUdabāᵓ* (Cairo, 1936), 12: 81–115.

8. ᶜUthmān Ibn Jinnī, *Al-Khaṣāᵓiṣ*, 1:chaps. 10, 11, 12.

the jurists and the scholastic theologians had done in their disciplines.

There is another merit in the work accomplished by ʾAbū ʿAlī al-Fārisī and ʿUthmān Ibn Jinnī, which lies in their having placed the language under the creative and molding authority of reason, delivering it from the exclusive domain of tradition where the attitude of man to his language could only be that of blind submission and pious reverence. This constructive role of the *qiyās* and the intellectual openness of its defenders will be one of the most precious heritages and attitudes taken over by the men of the *Nahḍah*. These men were deeply inspired and guided by this heritage in their efforts to revive and modernize the Arabic language. Thus the analogical method, in its different aspects, has been discussed and applied by men of the *Nahḍah* like Jurjī Zaydān,[9] Maḥmūd Shukrī al-ʾĀlūsī,[10] ʾAḥmad Taymūr,[11] Maʿrūf al-Ruṣāfī,[12] ʿAbd al-Qādir al-Maghribī,[13] Muṣṭafā Ṣādiq al-Rāfiʿī,[14] Sāṭiʿ al-Ḥuṣrī,[15] ʾAḥmad ʾAmīn,[16] ʾIsmāʿīl Maẓhar,[17] ʿAbd al-Lāh Nadīm,[18] Muṣṭafā Jawād,[19] and others.[20]

9. Jurjī Zaydān, *Al-Falsafah al-Lughawīyah wa al-ʾAlfāẓ al-ʿArabīyah*, rev. ed. (Cairo, 1961), pp. 59–66.

10. Maḥmūd Shukrī al-ʾĀlūsī, *Bulūgh al-ʾArab fī Maʿrifat ʾAḥwāl al-ʿArab*, 2d ed. (Cairo, 1923), 1:45–46.

11. ʾAḥmad Taymūr, *Al-Samāʿ wa al-Qiyās* (Cairo, 1955).

12. Muṣṭafā ʿAlī, *Muḥāḍarāt ʿan Maʿrūf al-Ruṣāfī* (Cairo, 1954), pp. 31–32.

13. ʿAbd al-Qādir al-Maghribī, *Kitāb al-Ishtiqāq wa al-Taʿrīb*, 2d ed. (Cairo, 1947).

14. Muṣṭafā Ṣādiq al-Rāfiʿī *Taʾrīkh ʾĀdāb al-ʿArab*, 3d ed. (Cairo, 1953), 1:169–215.

15. Sāṭiʿ al-Ḥuṣrī, *ʾĀrāʾ wa ʾAḥādīth fī al-Lughah wa al-ʾAdab* (Beirut, 1958), pp. 130–147.

16. ʾAḥmad ʾAmīn, *Ḍuḥā al-ʾIslām*, 5th ed. (Cairo, 1956), 2:243–318.

17. ʾIsmāʿīl Maẓhar, *Tajdīd al-ʿArabīyah* (Cairo, 1947).

18. ʿAbd al-Lāh Nadīm, *Al-Ishtiqāq* (Cairo, 1956).

19. Muṣṭafā Jawād, "Wasāʾil al-Nuhūḍ bi al-Lughah al-ʿArabīyah," in *Al-ʾUstādh*, 8 (1955):113–25.

20. Discussions of many of the problems related to the *qiyās* may be found in the *Majmaʿ al-Lughah al-ʿArabīyah. Maḥāḍir al-Jalasāt* [Minutes of the Royal Academy of the Arabic Language] (Cairo), hereafter cited as *Minutes*. See note 35 below.

Of these, probably the most dedicated to the cause of the modernization of the language and the most consistent exponent of the analogical principle is ᶜAbd al-Qādir al-Maghribī. His philosophy of the language has its roots in the early disputes over the origin of Arabic as the sacred language of the Koran. The dispute originated around the perplexing evidence of non-Arabic vocabulary in the Koran and soon developed into the fundamental question of whether Arabic is an inspired language, received by the first man in its perfection, or whether it is the product of human need for communication—in modern terms, whether it is an historical and sociological phenomenon. In the later part of the nineteenth century these problems had already been revived and discussed anew, but the question of the sacred origin of the Arabic language remained an issue even in the twenties of the present century.[21]

Al-Maghribī sees the language as a sociological organism whose growth and evolution are analogous to the growth and evolution of a people or nation. In the Arabic case, the nation formed itself out of two elements and along two paths: by natural increase of the autochthonous population inside the Arab ethnic group (*al-tawālud*), and by assimilation of non-Arabic elements (*al-tajannus*). In a similar way, Arabic language emerged, grew, and should continue to grow both by derivation from Arabic roots (*al-ishtiqāq*, which is analogous to *al-tawālud*), and by assimilation of foreign vocabulary (*al-taᶜrīb*, which would correspond to *al-tajannus*). Thus, there is an organic equation between *tawālud* and *ishtiqāq*, as well as between *tajannus* and *taᶜrīb*.[22]

In discussing authoritatively the entire scope of the problem, this sociological treatment of the language runs the danger of colliding with traditional theological concepts (we must remember that al-Maghribī's work was written in 1908), because of the inevitable allusion to words of foreign origin—the *al-taᶜrīb*—in the Koran. It

21. Ṭaha Ḥusayn, *Ḥadīth al-ʾArbaᶜāʾ* (Cairo, 1957), 3:29, 33.
22. Al-Maghribī, *Al-Ishtiqāq*, pp. 6–7.

is written in the Koran: *ʾInnā ʾanzalnāhu qurʾānan ʿarabīyan.*[23] Al-Maghribī only avoids this danger by arguing that *al-taʿrīb*, meaning arabization, should not interfere with the authority of the Koranic verse, but should rather harmonize with it.[24] Having paid tribute to tradition, al-Maghribī can proceed with his own exposition, whose broad structure we shall keep in mind for the present discussion.

DERIVATION FROM ROOTS ORIGINALLY ARABIC (*AL-ISHTIQĀQ*)

Derivation from existing Arabic roots has always been considered the most natural way of growth for the language. Arabic has been called the language of *ishtiqāq*, and this ability to grow from its own essence has given the language its rare homogeneousness, which is the pride of Arab writers and philologists and which they are zealous to protect.[25] Classical Arabic philology distinguishes three main forms of derivation: the simple or "small" derivation (*al-ishtiqāq al-ṣaghīr*); the metathesis (*qalb*) or "large" derivation (*al-ishtiqāq al-kabīr*); and the root transformation (*ʾibdāl*) or "largest" derivation (*al-ishtiqāq al-ʾakbar*).

1. THE SIMPLE DERIVATION

The simple derivation is the only form of derivation which remained fully operative after the formative stage of the Arabic language. Here the radical consonants are not changed in any way, but are derived from and built upon. The original example of this derivation is, of course, the simple declension, such as *faʿala—yafʿalu—fāʿilun—mafʿūlun*, and so on.

In the process of the creation of new vocabulary, the simple derivation has played the most prominent role. Its

23. Koran, Sura XII, 2.

24. Al-Maghribī, *Al-Ishtiqāq*, pp. 6–7. This explanation of al-Maghribī's is evidently based on the summary of this topic given by Ibn Fāris in his *Al-Ṣāḥibī* (Cairo, 1910), pp. 28–30, or upon the parallel quotation contained in the *Al-ʾItqān* of al-Suyūṭī. See *Al-ʾItqān* (Cairo, 1951), 1:137.

25. As, for example, al-Rāfiʿī, *Taʾrīkh ʾĀdāb al-ʿArab* (Cairo, 1953), 1:169; or al-ʾĀlūsī, *Bulūgh al-ʾArab* (Cairo, 1923), 1:45.

use, in accordance with the principle of analogy, was practically uninterrupted throughout the history of the Arabic language. In the first Abbasid period it helped to create the enormous scope of scientific terminology for practically all the sciences that were originally Arabic or assimilated. Thus the terminology of entire fields, such as philology, philosophy, and, of course, theology, are indebted almost exclusively to this form of *ishtiqāq*. In early medieval times new strata of derivations were added to the already existing vocabulary. At times these derivations overstepped the classical limits of *qiyās*, as, for example, the secondary derivation of the verb *tamadhhaba* from the primarily derived noun *madhhab*. Mostly, however, such derivations only emphasized an existing possibility, as in the case of the *nisbah* formation of abstract nouns through the adding of a final *īyah* or *ānīyah*. Thus were coined *shuᶜūbīyah* (a movement deemphasizing the Arab hegemony), *huwīyah* (essence, nature), *māhīyah* (quality, essence), *kayfīyah* (qualification), *rūḥānīyah* (spirituality), and others.[26] It is safe to assert, however, that the most flourishing age of the principle of derivation by analogy is the one which started in the present *Nahḍah*, and which is still gaining in strength.

The formalized, abstract structure of the Arabic language is uniquely suited for the application of the analogical method of derivation. In theory, a simple triliteral root

26. For early examples of the use of *huwīyah*, *māhīyah*, and also of *hādhīyah*, see al-Jāḥiẓ, *Al-Bayān wa al-Tabyīn* (Cairo, 1960), 1:139; for *rūḥānīyah* see Vincent Monteil, *L'arabe moderne* (Paris, 1960), pp. 122–23, together with his reference to L. Massignon. Otherwise, it should be noticed that a term like *rūḥānīyah* is first of all characteristically *ṣūfī*, and as such it is frequently used by Ibn ᶜArabī (died A.H. 638), as, for example, in his *Tarjumān al-ᵓAshwāq* (Beirut, 1961), p. 15: "Wa kānat taghlibu ᶜalayhā al-rūḥānīyah." But a fully equivalent use to the modern one of the adjective *rūḥānī* can be found in non-*ṣūfī* literature as well. Thus in the Andalusian Ibn Shuhayd (died A.H. 426): ". . . bi mawādda rūḥānīyah" (*Risālat al-Tawābiᶜ wa al-Zawābiᶜ* [Beirut, 1951], p. 118); or in ᶜAbd al-Qāhir al-Jurjānī (died A.H. 471): "ᵓumūr khafīfah wa maᶜānin rūḥānīyah," from *Dalāᵓil al-ᵓIᶜjāz*, as quoted by Muḥammad Mandūr, *Al-Naqd al-Manhajī ᶜinda al-ᶜArab* (Cairo, 1948), p. 286.

offers almost inexhaustible possibilities. The some forty-four verbal nouns which could be derived from the ground form of a hypothetically used triliteral verb (*faᶜala*) should alone be a convincing, although startling, example of this purely theoretical flexibility of Arabic.[27]

Such vast possibilities of derivation, however, are limited in one way which reflects upon the substance and nature of Arabic, since, according to classical rules, derivations should be made from verbal roots only. Thus the verb lies formally at the basis of the Arabic *ishtiqāq*. In spite of linguistic evidence to the contrary, evidence showing that the noun may lie at the basis of a verbal derivation, classical Arabic philology would not allow the criterion of *qiyās* to be applied to this latter possibility or dimension of the language.[28]

Abstract nouns which implicitly refer to verbal ideas of action or state are derived from ground verbs containing these ideas. The same is true of concrete nouns denoting the agent or the effect of an act. Even onomatopoeic concrete nouns would have to be excluded from the nonderived category. All the verbal derivations referring to such nouns are not recognized as stemming from them but rather as sharing one common root. The nouns which may not be derived from are themselves nonderived, and therefore they lack the ground root which would make derivation possible. Nouns of non-Arabic origin like *sijill*, *ward*, *minjanīq*, are nonderived as well.

Many primary concrete nouns, however, have defied the rule and have developed their own verbal derivatives,

27. W. Wright, *A Grammar of the Arabic Language*, 3rd ed. (Cambridge, 1955), 1:110–12.

28. This position is maintained only with regard to actual derivation by analogy (*ishtiqāq*). As far as the classical grammarians' views on the origins of the language are concerned, the noun or the *maṣdar* may be accepted as the primary element and the verb as the secondary derivative (as by some Basrans); or the nontemporal or "permansive" *al-fiᶜl al-dāʾim* may be laid at the basis of verbal derivations (as by the Kufans). These problems are fairly comprehensively reviewed by al-Makhzūmī in *Fī al-Naḥw al-ᶜArabī*, pp. 103–5, 144–45.

as, for example, *rijl-rajila*, *ʾasad-istaʾsada*, *Najd-ʾanjada*;[29] or *sijill-sajjala*, *ward-tawarrada*, *minjanīq-janaqa*. Such evidence, however, is not to be considered analogically normative, and the rule of *al-bāb al-mughlaq* (the "closed door" or "category") is to be applied so as to prevent a further proliferation of this linguistic "accident."

In modern times we find among the first tasks of the Academy of the Arabic Language the attempt to investigate the theoretical basis of the classical attitude to this problem, with opening the "closed door" a possible result. Significant preliminary studies were done in this respect by ʾAḥmad ʿAlī al-ʾIskandarī and by Ḥanafī Nāṣif.[30] The examples provided by these scholars, although numerous, were largely known to ancient grammarians as well. Only al-ʾIskandarī's recognition of secondary concrete nouns like *mankib* (shoulder) and of independent verbal derivations from them (*tanakkaba*) constitutes a fresh view of the problem.[31] The official philological attitude, as represented by the Royal Academy of the Arabic Language (Cairo), remained none the less reluctant. Analogical derivation from concrete nouns became sanctioned in "scientific language" only.[32]

Considering the Arabic system of word derivation as a whole, it becomes clear that the possibilities of noun derivation are much more numerous and diversified than those of verbal derivation. At least theoretically, the verbal derivation is limited to the standard fifteen forms—always maintaining the premise of a basic verbal root as the initial point of any verbal derivative. Thus, within the purely theoretical possibilities of derivation from any triliteral

29. Ultimately, *Najd*, too, is a derivation. Notwithstanding, *ʾanjada* may be considered as a primary derivation from the place name and not from the root meaning.

30. See a reference to their contribution, as well as further discussion of the topic, in *Minutes*, 1:354; see also the extensive list of examples in al-ʾIskandarī's paper in *Majallat Majmaʿ al-Lughah al-ʿArabīyah* (1934), 1:236–68.

31. *Majallat Majmaʿ al-Lughah al-ʿArabīyah*, 1:236.

32. Ibid., p. 235.

root, an extremely small percentage of derived words[33] would be verbs, with the rest falling into the broad category of the Arabic noun. In practice, however, verbal derivations may constitute between 10 and 25 percent of a given root.

Live linguistic practice and the theoretical capacity for derivation by analogy have maintained a harmonious balance in the history of the development of the Arabic language. A polarized and schematic presentation of the grammatical schools of Basra and Kufa could easily create an exaggerated impression of tension and strife, of a struggle for hegemony between analogy and linguistic habit. This extreme view of the problem is far from the truth, however. Seen from the perspective of time and within a broader frame of historical development of Arabic philological thought and linguistic practice, the two schools appear, rather, to supplement each other. The criterion of *qiyās* was normative more than it was formative. Its categorical application, although envisioned, was never carried through methodically. The methodical and abstract study of *qiyās* as a formative criterion in the growth of the language should be considered as a product of the Arabic philological revival which is taking place in the present. Whereas in the past derivation of new terms rested in the hands of individuals confronted with restricted linguistic problems, and *qiyās* still operated as the "spirit of the language," in the present the problem of new vocabulary has become totally engrossing, massive, and urgent, and the linguistic effort has become increasingly organized. Classical Arabic civilization was largely creative of its own standards and values, and the growth of the language had but to keep pace with the gradual development of that civilization. Thus it was an organic, harmonious growth: a civilization growing within a language, and a language engulfing a civilization.

The modern challenge to Arabic was of a different nature. The total onslaught of a highly developed, immensely

33. In the Arabic case it would be more appropriate to use the term *qawālib* (molds), since it reflects better the abstract nature of Arabic derivation by analogy.

ramified, extraneous civilization left no time for slow, natural processes of assimilation. A total challenge could be met successfully only by a total response. Fortunately enough, Arabic, with its lexical wealth and its characteristic morphological flexibility as regards derivation, is—in theory at least—well equipped to meet this challenge in several equally promising ways, one of which is the categorical application of the criterion of derivation by analogy. To modern Arabic cultural institutions like the academies, as well as to individual writers and linguists concerned with the modernization of the language, the criterion of *qiyās* became dynamically formative and not merely a normative harness. Furthermore, this criterion went beyond being a largely subconscious "spirit of the language," and became a rational, clearly purposeful proposition.

This new, scientific attitude is probably best illustrated by the Egyptian engineer and amateur linguist, Ḥasan Ḥusayn Fahmī, as he exploits the capacity for derivation of the root *ṣahara* (to melt, liquefy, fuse).[34] Ḥasan Ḥusayn Fahmī offers a list of derivatives from this root amounting to some 196 lexical items, divided into verbs and nouns and based on the full scale of the derivational verbal molds. The remarkable thing about this list is that each one of the individual derivatives actually possesses a clear and usable meaning. Ḥasan Ḥusayn Fahmī, however, applies his derivations from *ṣahara* to metallurgy only, without taking into consideration further semantic possibilities of this root, already fixed by early linguistic habit. This produces some overlapping of meaning which could lead to confusion in instances where the language of technology is used outside of its strictly scientific context.

Not quite as implacably methodic, yet much more ramified, is the work of the various committees of the

34. See his interesting, although frequently plagued by inexactitudes, *Al-Marjiᶜ fī Taᶜrīb al-Muṣṭalaḥāt al-ᶜIlmīyah wa al-Fannīyah wa al-Handasīyah* (Cairo, 1958), pp. 338–45. This book, which appeared under the aegis of the Academy of the Arabic Language (Cairo) and was prefaced by Ṭaha Ḥusayn, could easily have been saved from its amateurish presentation.

Arab academicians of Cairo and Damascus.[35] The role of these committees is to gather lexical material pertaining to the sciences, the arts, as well as to the broad spectrum of "vocabulary of modern civilization and daily life," and to present their findings for ratification by the sessions of the academies. Specific linguistic problems are ruled upon by the academies through decrees or resolutions (*qarārāt*). These rulings should then serve as directions for lexicography as well as for the general literary use of the language.[36]

Aside from the corporate effort of the academies and from such methodic assaults on specific fields as the one exemplified by Ḥasan Ḥusayn Fahmī, there remains the work of innumerable known or anonymous contributors to the modern Arabic lexicon. This individual, often extemporaneous effort, has its roots in the early movement of translation which began in Egypt under Muḥammad ᶜAlī, as well as in the rapidly developing periodical press, centered in Egypt and in Lebanon. The translators and the

35. The former Royal Academy of Cairo, now the Academy of the Arabic Language (*Majmaᶜ al-Lughah al-ᶜArabīyah*), was founded in 1932 and publishes a *Minutes* and *Journal*. The Arab Academy of Damascus (*Al-Majmaᶜ al-ᶜIlmī al-ᶜArabī*), founded in 1921, publishes a *Journal*. There had been earlier attempts at founding an Arab academy. In 1892, a group of scholars had founded in Cairo, in the fashion of an academy, a circle concerned with linguistic matters. In 1907, the scholars of Dār al-ᶜUlūm (Cairo) made a similar attempt. A more permanent achievement has been the journal *Lughat al-ᶜArab*, founded in 1911 in Baghdad by Anastase-Marie de Saint-Elie. This journal can justly be considered as the Iraqi equivalent of the publications of the Cairo and Damascus academies.

36. In its fourteenth session (held on February 18, 1934), the Royal Academy of the Arabic Language (Cairo) established a special committee, called *Lajnat al-ᵓUṣūl al-ᶜĀmmah*. This committee was to investigate the rules and linguistic foundations of Arabic and present its findings to the Academy, which would adopt them for further, detailed debate, with a view towards issuing authoritative definitions and binding recommendations. The topics which the committee was to investigate were: 1) the implied use of verbs and the substitution of prepositions (*al-taḍmīn fī al-ᵓafᶜāl wa niyābat al-ḥurūf*); 2) word coinage (*al-tawlīd*); 3) derivation; 4) arabization or assimilation of foreign vocabulary. Having scrutinized and established the methods of work, the Academy would create separate committees for each branch of the sciences and for each environmental aspect of life and society. See *Minutes*, 1:182–92.

journalists, taken together, have thus far produced and fixed in live usage many more neologisms than the academies. As the healthy growth of modern Arabic continues, there should come a time when the Arab academies will be able to assume a natural, normative role only, one of watchfulness over the purity of a language which will not be of their making in the narrow sense. It is fair to remark that most of the individual effort, too, rests on the sound linguistic basis of derivation by analogy.

The unorganized, individual, and sporadic contribution to the modern enrichment of the Arabic language is most difficult to trace in detail without a meticulous lexical study of early *Nahḍah* literary material. A view at the organized effort in this respect is much simpler, since it provides us with general guidelines taken over from classical Arabic philology. The publications of the Arab academies of Cairo and Damascus are particularly illuminating as regards the theoretical premises of this linguistic enterprise.

Thus, in the practical application of the analogical method of derivation, we find the organizing criterion to be that of the linguistic molds or *qawālib*. All neologisms have to obey this criterion.

With regard to the verb, it should be possible to obtain new derivatives with their respective meanings (causative, factitive, reflexive, of mutual action or effect, putative, and so on) only in accordance with the abstract meaning implied in each one of the corresponding verbal *qawālib*. These verbal *qawālib* possess inherent meanings which are sufficiently well defined, besides being manageable in number. This allows an almost unerring application of *qiyās* in verbal derivation.

As regards the derivation of nouns, however, there the variety of linguistic molds is too great to allow a fully normative application of the *qiyās*. As a result, it becomes impossible to achieve a clearly differentiated, comprehensive series of independent nouns, derived from one single root, where each semantic item would correspond to a basic semantic dimension in the respective mold, and where the entire scale of the nominal molds would be applied unequivocally. A selective approach to the Arabic noun derivation, therefore, becomes necessary. A theoretical tour de force, like the one carried through by Ḥasan Ḥusayn Fahmī,[37] may be attempted with regard to some particularly yielding roots, but such an approach can not be considered a viable criterion on a larger scale.

In our discussion of the application of the method of analogy, we shall treat separately the nominal and the verbal forms, although it will become clear that, particularly in the case of the verbal derivations, the existence of the infinitive verbal noun creates ambiguous situations of usage, where the infinitive may serve as an indication that the corresponding verbal form either exists or may be brought into existence as a stylistic substitute for the nominal form.

The derived noun

The Royal Academy of the Arabic Language in Cairo had attempted to define the nominal *qawālib* in order to study the possibility of their analogical application to neologisms. This study was never completed, and only a few of the more frequently occurring *qawālib* were actually discussed and recommended as applicable practically.[38]

Thus, the mold *fiᶜālah* should be used for terms denoting profession or type of activity, like *ṣināᶜah* (industry), *ṭibāᶜah* (art of printing), *sifārah* (embassy), *jirāḥah* (surgery), *ṣiḥāfah*—also *ṣaḥāfah* (journalism), and the like.

The mold *faᶜalān* should be applied in intransitive verbs for terms denoting fluctuating movement or commotion, like *mawajān* (in connection with electronics—stream or fluctuation), *sayalān* (liquefaction), *ṭayarān* (aviation), and so on.

The mold *fuᶜāl* should be applied for terms denoting

37. See above, p. 12.

38. See *Minutes*, 1 (January 1934–March 1934): 415–18; *Minutes*, 2 (February 1935–April 1935): 7–8; *Majallat Majmaᶜ al-Lughah al-ᶜArabīyah al-Malakī*, 1:206–16.

sickness, such as *suᶜāl* (cough),[39] *zukām* (cold, catarrh), *judhām* (leprosy), and as in the neologism *nukāf* (parotitis).[40]

The mold *faᶜᶜāl* is to be used in deriving terms which denote profession or characterize habitual activity, such as *jarrāḥ* (surgeon), *ṭayyār* (pilot), *sawwāq* (chauffeur).

In the early sessions, the Cairo Academy showed particular interest in defining the analogical application of the molds denoting nouns of instrument (*ʾasmāʾ al-ʾālah*), which are three: *mifᶜal, mifᶜāl,* and *mifᶜalah.* The Academy's discussion was centered around the classical definitions of these molds. According to some philologists the mold *mifᶜalah* should not be applied analogically. Besides, only triradical roots were considered as admitting the application of these molds. The biradical *ʾasmāʾ al-ʾālah,* even though existing in profusion and recognized as fully classical, were not to be treated as permitting analogy. The academicians ᶜAbd al-Qādir al-Maghribī and Manṣūr Fahmī, however, insisted that sound as well as defective, transitive as well as intransitive, verbs may form such nouns analogically.[41] Classical grammarians treated such derivations from intransitive verbs as individual cases sanctioned by usage only (*samāᶜī*). A modern derivation of this kind would be the word *midfaʾah* (stove), now accepted by current literary usage.

The Cairo Academy found it difficult to rule on the

39. The mold *fuᶜāl* denotes also sound, and therefore *suᶜāl* could also be included among nouns of sound, like *nubāḥ* (barking). The mold *faᶜīl* has also been accepted as analogically applicable. See above: p. 15 (footnote 38).

40. (*Majmūᶜat*) *al-Buḥūth wa al-Muḥāḍarāt—Majmaᶜ al-Lughah al-ᶜArabīyah* (Cairo, 1961), 3:257–60. See the list of *fuᶜāl*-type neologisms approved by the Cairo Academy in 1961. On the basis of the proposed examples, and in accordance with an older ruling (1934) which allows derivation from concrete nouns, a new, supplementary ruling of the Academy provided that terms denoting diseases may be derived from concrete nouns etymologically relevant to the respective disease, such as *fuyāl* (elephantiasis) from *fīl* (elephant); *ẓulāf* (hoof-disease) from *ẓilf* (cloven hoof); and the like. In this ruling, the Academy also sanctions the mold *faᶜal* to be used as an alternate for *fuᶜāl.*

41. *Minutes,* 1:359–60.

subject of the *ʾasmāʾ al-ʾālah*. After adjournments and reconsiderations, the Academy finally ruled that all three molds (*mifʿal, mifʿāl, mifʿalah*) may be analogically applied to triradical verbal roots.[42] This ruling, which did not exclude intransitive verbs, however, continued to be disputed, and never became formally ratified by the Academy.

In modern linguistic practice, the molds denoting instruments have found the widest possible application, since the general linguistic sense concerning their inherent meaning had never lost the necessary precision. This well-defined meaning-dimension allows even spontaneous word-coinage, which, however, need not be felt as totally arbitrary.

Characteristic examples of neologisms actually coined this way, and now generally accepted, are *mijhar* (microscope), *miṣʿad* (elevator), *mijhār* (loudspeaker), *midhyāʿ* (microphone, but also broadcasting station), *mirwaḥah* (propeller),[43] *misarrah* (speaking tube, telephone).[44]

This avenue of methodical definition of the nominal *qawālib* did not take the academic innovators of the language very far, however, because most of these *qawālib* eluded such strict methodology. A more general consensus was reached by those dealing with neologisms—within the academies as well as without. It was agreed that the

42. Ibid., p. 397.

43. For "propeller" Hans Wehr (*A Dictionary of Modern Written Arabic* [Ithaca, N.Y., 1961]) also lists *dāsir*. Thus far this latter term does not seem to have gained any acceptance at all, and other dictionaries of modern Arabic do not list it.

44. In search for a concise equivalent of "motor of internal combustion," the Cairo Academy proposed in 1934, instead of the calque *ʾālat al-iḥtirāq al-dākhilī*, the terms *miḥdām* or *miḥdamah*, both derived from the root *ḥadama* (to burn, to blaze; to boil fiercely, pot). Equally, the Academy suggested as synonymous two derivatives from the root *warā* (to kindle): *wāriyah* and *ʾāriyah*, obtained according to the mold *fāʿilah*. None of these four terms has gained acceptance. The methodic procedure of the Academy remains as the only thing of interest in this case. See *Majallat Majmaʿ al-Lughah al-ʿArabīyah al-Malakī*, 1 (1935): 119–21. The term *misarrah*, which until now has remained only marginally used, had been suggested as early as 1892 by the short-lived Academy which met that year in Cairo. See ʾAnwar al-Jundī, *Al-Lughah al-ʿArabīyah bayna Ḥumātihā wa Khuṣūmihā* (Cairo, n.d.), p. 53.

coining of new vocabulary should proceed according to three principles, which fall essentially into the realm of *ishtiqāq*. These principles are:

—actual derivation from existing roots;

—derivation through approximation of older vocabulary to new meanings, either through figurative semantic extension (*al-waḍᶜ bi al-majāz*) or through the revival of archaic vocabulary (*gharīb al-lughah*) which has been given contemporary, not necessarily directly related, meanings.

—coining of neologisms by means of the so-called *al-ishtiqāq al-maᶜnawī* or *al-ishtiqāq bi al-tarjamah*, which consists in the translation of foreign terms, that is, in their descriptive paraphrasis.

A discussion of these three principles, together with a selective list of neologisms that fall under each, should give the reader an idea of how theory and practice mingle, or how practice very often outweighs theory in this collective effort to modernize the Arabic language.

Actual derivation of new terms from existing roots

This is not always as clear a principle as may be assumed. Many neologisms based formally on this principle might as well fall into the category of words coined through semantic extension in the broad sense, particularly where conceptualization and abstraction are concerned; or they may represent the principle of figurative semantic extension (*al-waḍᶜ bi al-majāz*). The latter then boils down to a more arbitrary and forced use of ancient words for new purposes. The important aspect of semantic extension, as concerns conceptualization and abstraction in the true sense, will not be treated in detail within the context of *ishtiqāq*, since it will be allotted special attention in a separate chapter. Only the formal similarities between old words and their new meanings will be duly referred to.

Examples of simple derivation have already been given in connection with the methodic application of nominal linguistic molds. Some of those examples constitute new derivations in the true sense, others are in reality the products of *al-waḍᶜ bi al-majāz*. Thus, *ṣināᶜah* already possessed the related meaning of "craft," "art." The modern meaning of *ṭibāᶜah*, however, has little to do with the art of sword manufacturing, which is the classical meaning of that word. As "art of printing," it is thus a derivation from the root-meaning, which is "to seal," "to imprint [with a seal]." The term *ṣiḥāfah* is a derivation from the concrete noun *ṣaḥīfah* (sheet to write on), which, through a process of *al-waḍᶜ bi al-majāz,* acquired the modern meaning of "newspaper."[45]

Looking at examples from other molds, we see that *nukāf*, with its modern meaning of "parotitis," is an extension of the old term for "tumor on a camel's jaw," itself derived from the concrete noun *nakfatāni* (dual—two projecting bones of a camel's jaw).

The classical meaning of *sawwāq* is "driver of cattle." In this case the modern meaning (chauffeur) is both a formal derivation from the verbal root *sāqa* and a figurative extension of the old term.

A curious etymological process can be observed in the neologisms *mijhar* and *mijhār*. The root *jahara* (to become exceedingly perceptible, either visually or acoustically) is common to both terms. *Mijhar*, as "microscope," represents a regular derivation from the root-meaning. The term *mijhār* (loudspeaker), however, is in a direct fashion a figurative extension of the classical meaning: "s. o. who speaks with a plain and clear voice," "someone who speaks in public." As such, *mijhār* is a noun of instrument in a remote, etymological sense only. In an immediate sense, it is an intensive adjectival form, denoting almost exactly the modern meaning of "loudspeaker," extended from a person to an instrument, and thus retaining the intensive

45. The modern semantic history of *ṣiḥāfah* and *ṣaḥīfah* has been traced by ᵓAdīb Murūwah in his book *Al-Ṣiḥāfah al-ᶜArabīyah: Nashᵓatuhā wa Taṭawwuruhā* (Beirut, 1961), pp. 13–15. Rashīd al-Daḥdaḥ (1813–1894) was the one who gave the word *ṣaḥīfah* its modern meaning. From this new term, the writer and journalist Najīb al-Ḥaddād (1867–1899) derived the word *ṣiḥāfah* in its present meaning (journalism). From *ṣiḥāfah* was then derived the adjectival *ṣiḥāfī* (journalist), while from *ṣaḥīfah* was derived the parallel, less correct although more current, *ṣuḥufī* (*ṣaḥafī* would have been the proper form, since *faᶜīlah* gives the *nisbah* adjective *faᶜalī*).

adjectival meaning, yet becoming, in an archaic fashion, formally a noun of instrument.

The modern term *miṣᶜad* (elevator) should be regarded as a simple derivative of its verbal root, although there exists the related classical derivative *miṣᶜād* (an instrument—a hoop—for climbing palm-trees).

The original meaning of *mirwaḥah* is "fan," of which "propeller" is a modern figurative extension.

On the basis of this discussion of a few neologisms only, we may already see some of the complexities involved in the workings of the method of derivation. Even the authenticity of the concept of primary derivation, as it is designated by the Arabic term *al-ishtiqāq al-ṣaghīr*, if tested methodologically, is not always beyond contention. The mixture of formal primary derivation and secondary semantic extension or superposition, however, very often issues harmoniously from an active linguistic sense for morphological possibilities, together with the permanence of a concrete lexical memory. Such a mixture or interaction is particularly natural in Arabic, where the concept of etymology involves both the concrete semantic history of a word and its reduction to a linguistic abstraction within the formal scheme of derived molds.

Since what is intended on these pages is only a representative discussion of the characteristic processes in modern Arabic lexical innovations, lengthy lists of neologisms which fall into our present category will be avoided. This task has to be left to historical lexicography. For the sake of adequate illustration it should suffice to mention a few of the most frequently occurring nominal, participial, and adjectival molds which lend themselves to analogical derivation theoretically as well as out of a natural linguistic sense common to all alert users of the language.

From the molds designating locality (*mafᶜal, mafᶜil, mafᶜalah*), many neologisms have been obtained, some of them derivations in the full sense, others semantic extensions:

maṣnaᶜ (factory)—could be considered as a semantic extension

maṭbaᶜ (printing house, press)—remotely a semantic extension

majmaᶜ (academy)—a semantic extension, originally "a place of gathering"

masraḥ (stage, theatre)[46]

maᵓsāh (tragedy)—a straight modern derivation from the verbal root[47]

maqṣaf (buffet, refreshment room)—derived from an already postclassical root-meaning as a non-literary term, and then newly defined by ᵓIbrāhīm al-Yāzijī[48]

maṭār (airport)—a semantic extension, the classical meaning being "a place from which, or to which, a bird flies"

mawqif (stop, station; bus, train)—a semantic extension

maḥaṭṭah (station; railroad, broadcasting)—a semantic extension, the old meaning being: "a place where something (a load) is put down," "a place where one alights"

The mold *faᶜᶜālah*, designating an instrument or machine, or a place where something is produced, has found a very wide application in modern derivation as well. The basic emphatic adjectival function of the masculine form of this mold provides the connotation of constant, habitual action. Related to *faᶜᶜālah* is the mold *fāᶜilah*.

The following examples will illustrate the application of both molds:

sayyārah (automobile)[49]

dabbābah (tank)—a semantic extension of the medieval war-machine "testudo"

46. For a discussion of this term, see below, p. 47.

47. This term was coined by ᵓIbrāhīm al-Yāzijī (according to his own claim). See Fuᵓād ᵓIfrām al-Bustānī, *Al-Shaykh ᵓIbrāhīm al-Yāzijī: Fī al-Lughah wa al-ᵓAdab* (Beirut, 1952), p. 35.

48. Ibid., p. 35.

49. This neologism was proposed by ᵓAḥmad Zakī Pasha (1866–1934) in 1892. Other proposed terms for automobile—like *farrārah*—were rejected. See al-Jundī, *Al-ᶜArabīyah bayna Ḥumātihā wa Khuṣūmihā* (Cairo, n.d.), p. 53; also: *Minutes*, 1:450.

ḥarrāqah	(torpedo)—a semantic extension of the medieval "fireship"[50]
naffāthah	(jet plane)[51]
barrādah	(refrigerator, icebox)—a semantic extension of the old term for a vessel for cooling water, or a stand upon which vessels are put for cooling
thallājah	(icebox, freezer; also synonym of *barrādah*)—a primary derivation from the root-meaning
dabbāsah	(stapler)[52]
ṭāʾirah	(airplane)[53]
bākhirah	(steamship)
shāḥinah	(freighter; truck, lorry)
ḥāfilah	(bus)[54]

Most other nominal, adjectival, and participial molds can, and very frequently do, yield neologisms. The transparency of the inherent meanings diminishes in a great number of these molds, however, and, consequently, the regularity of their *ishtiqāq*-application disappears. By and large, therefore, certain molds produce neologisms of an extemporaneous nature. The phenomenon of semantic ex-

50. This term was suggested in 1892, soon after the invention of the device itself. See al-Jundī, *Al-ʿArabīyah bayna Ḥumātihā wa Khuṣūmihā*, pp. 52–53.

51. This neologism has a very characteristic history. It appeared in print for the first time in the journal *Al-Mukhtār* (July 1944). The article containing it, a translation from English, was entitled "Al-Ṭāʾirah al-Naffāthah Ṭāʾirat al-Mustaqbal." The editor of the journal and the translator of that particular article was Fuʾād Ṣarrūf. The interesting story of the coining of this term, as well as of a series of other terms, is told by Fuʾād Ṣarrūf himself in the article entitled "Siyar ʾAlfāẓ ʿArabīyah Mustaḥdathah," *Al-ʾAbḥāth* 16, no. 3 (September 1963): 281–98.

52. This neologism does not seem to figure in modern dictionaries yet. It was registered by Maḥmūd Taymūr in *Majmaʿ al-Lughah al-ʿArabīyah—Al-Buḥūth wa al-Muḥāḍarāt* (Cairo, 1961), 3:117.

53. The form *faʿʿālah* of this root (*ṭayyārah*) has come to mean "aviatrix." Notice, however, that in the colloquial languages the basic mold of *faʿʿālah* has prevailed in the derivation of a term for "airplane": *ṭayyārah* (Eg.), *ṭiyyārah* (Ir.).

54. This term appears to have been first used by ʾAḥmad Fāris al-Shidyāq (1805–1887). Maḥmūd Taymūr suggests as his first choice the term *sayyārah ʿāmmah*. See his paper, entitled "ʾAlfāẓ al-Ḥaḍārah," in *Majmaʿ al-Lughah al-ʿArabīyah—Majmūʿat al-Buḥūth wa al-Muḥāḍarāt* (Cairo, 1960), vol. 2.

tension is even more frequent in such impromptu derivations.

A few examples should suffice to illustrate this diversity of approaches to derivation:

shaṭīrah (sandwich).[55] This term originated in the Cairo Academy (Massignon), with the root *shaṭara* used in a humorously elaborate fashion to describe the appearance of a sandwich.

ᶜamīl (business representative; political agent; client). The pejorative connotation which this term may have is seen in the expression *al-intihāzī al-ᶜamīl* (the opportunistic lackey).[56]

ᶜamīd (dean). In classical Arabic the word means, among other things, "a person to resort to," "chief."

ratīb (monotonous). This modern meaning can eventually be related to the classical one, as in *ᵓamr ratīb* (a continual, uninterrupted affair). The connotation of annoyance and vexation which the modern term contains may have existed already in another classical derivative from the same root: *ratab* (difficulty, fatigue, weariness, embarrassment). The first lexicographer of modern Arabic, Ellious Bocthor, registers, instead, the following Arabic equivalents: *bārid, muzaᶜᶜal, bāsil.*[57]

gharīr (naive, inexperienced). Aside from the main meaning of "deceived," this word had already developed in classical Arabic the marginal meaning of "good disposition," "harmlessness."[58]

55. Used smoothly and effectively by Najīb Maḥfūẓ in his novel *Al-Ṭarīq* (Cairo, 1964).

56. See Kamāl Junblāt, *Fī Majrā al-Siyāsah al-Lubnānīyah: ᵓAwḍāᶜ wa Takhṭīṭ* (Beirut, 1959), p. 57. The pejorative connotation of *ᶜamila* is also apparent in the substantive *ᶜamlah* (evil deed).

57. Ellious Bocthor, *Dictionnaire français-arabe,* rev. by Caussin de Perceval, 2d ed. (Paris, 1848), p. 513. See the comment upon the modern poetic use of *ratīb* by Nāzik al-Malāᵓikah in ᵓIbrāhīm al-Sāmarrāᵓī, *Lughat al-Shiᶜr bayna Jīlayn* (Beirut, n.d.), p. 187.

58. Similarly to the new meaning of *ratīb, gharīr,* too, has found

Participial molds of derived verbal forms yield an especially large number of neologisms. Particularly frequent are Form II derivatives:

muḥarrik (motor, engine)
muwallid (generator, dynamo)
mulawwan (colored, as referring to Negroes)[59]
mudarraj (amphitheatre, a similarly arranged auditorium)[60]

The use of participles of Form III, as designating the communication of something to someone else, and of Form VI for mutual communication or interaction, is fully classical, although the frequency with which such derivatives are used analogically today is much higher than in earlier periods. As a lesser known, but characteristic, example the term *mujālid* (gladiator) may serve; it was proposed by the Cairo Academy on the basis of its analogy with *muqātil*.[61] This term still awaits general acceptance in literary usage.

Passive participial nominal derivatives of Form VIII, with their connotation of locality, are most common in modern Arabic as well. They may designate either specific terms of common usage, or they may be dictated by individual contextual situations. In the latter case such derivatives do not necessarily represent common usage. Their conceptual transparency, however, indicates a lively sense for the analogical possibilities of the language.

---

convincing acceptance in modern poetry. See ʾAbū al-Qāsim al-Shābbī, *ʾAghānī al-Ḥayāh* (Cairo, 1955), p. 149.

59. For the use of this term in a work of fiction see Najīb Maḥfūẓ, *Qaṣr al-Shawq* (Cairo, 1957), p. 137; for its use in a work of publicity see Ḥamdī Ḥāfiẓ, *Al-Mulawwanūn fī al-Wilāyāt al-Muttaḥidah al-ʾAmrīkīyah* (Cairo, 1963).

60. This term was introduced by the Dār al-ʿUlūm group in 1907. See al-Jundī, *Al-ʿArabīyah bayna Ḥumātihā wa Khuṣūmihā*, p. 76. It became accepted to a certain degree, and it is foreseeable that it may establish itself completely. See its use by Najīb Maḥfūẓ in his novel *Al-Sarāb* (Cairo, 1958), p. 91. Side by side, however, the older arabicized word, *ʾanfitiyātir*, persists as the temporarily predominant term. Ḥasan Ḥusayn Fahmī would in such cases retain the arabicized phonetic transliteration. See his *Al-Marjiʿ*, p. 167.

61. *Minutes*, 3:264.

Characteristic examples of this group which have become specific terms are:

mustawan (level, niveau, standard). The noun is derived from the classical meaning of its verb, *istawā maᶜa* . . . (to become even or level with something). Ellious Bocthor registers only the *maṣdar* of Form III: *musāwāh* (*niveau, horizontalité*).[62] The semantic extension of an originally concrete meaning of *mustawan* is a recent development. As such the term is used both concretely and abstractly: *mustawā al-māᵓ* (waterlevel), *mustawā al-thaqāfah al-shaᶜbīyah* (level, standard of popular culture).[63]

mujtamaᶜ (society). The classical meaning of "gathering place" lies at the foundation of the modern terms.[64] Ellious Bocthor registers only *jamᶜīyah* and *ijtimāᶜīyah*.[65] It is only to be assumed that in the latter term Bocthor had in mind a fuller form of the same, *al-ḥayāh al-ijtimāᶜīyah*, as it appears in the usage of the later nineteenth century, as well as in dictionaries up to the thirties of the present century. The term *mujtamaᶜ* does not become current until some time around 1930.

mujtalad (arena). This neologism, proposed by the Cairo Academy in 1936,[66] is quoted here as an example of methodic application of this Form VIII mold. This particular term, however, did not become accepted in literary usage.

62. Bocthor, *Dictionnaire français-arabe*, p. 533.

63. Maḥmūd Taymūr offers a short list of the modern usages of *mustawan* in his "ᵓAlfāẓ al-Ḥaḍārah," in *Majmaᶜ al-Lughah al-ᶜArabīyah—Al-Buḥūth wa al-Muḥāḍarāt*, 3:130.

64. The geographer ᵓIdrīsī uses *mujtamaᶜ* with the meaning of "reunion," "assembly." See: R. Dozy, *Supplement aux dictionnaires arabes* (Leiden, 1881), p. 217.

65. Bocthor, *Dictionnaire français-arabe*, p. 761.

66. *Minutes*, 3:263–64. The brief discussion over the meaning of "arena," as well as over the Arabic term *mujtalad*, offers a good example of the Academy's approach to lexical problems.

An example of a not necessarily current, but contextually transparent, application of the above treated mold (*mufta^cal*) would be the derivative *al-mujtalā*, as it is used by the novelist Najīb Maḥfūẓ: "Kānat qahwat ʾAḥmad ʿAbduh . . . mujtalan li al-mutaʾammil" (. . . a place of contemplation, a revelation, for the pensive one).[67]

Aside from this sampling of specific molds which, with their pronounced inherent connotations, facilitate modern derivations which reflect such "generic" connotations, one should be warned that the modern process of semantic enrichment of the Arabic language extends across all forms and molds in a lively and apparently formally undisciplined fashion.

Abstract neologisms with their recourse to applicable *maṣdar* forms still preserve a pattern of linguistic reasoning, however. The *maṣdar* neologisms, too, as a rule, are semantic extensions rather than completely new words. Thus in the case of:

irtisāmāt (impressions), as in *irtisāmāt mughtarib* (impressions of an expatriate).[68]

tablīd (acclimatization), coined, apparently, by ʾIbrāhīm al-Yāzijī.[69]

taʾalluq (phosphorescence), also suggested by ʾIbrāhīm al-Yāzijī.[70]

taṣallub (intolerance). As such, this term was coined by the Cairo Academy in 1936. A more current term for "intolerance," however, as it was at the time the Academy was busy with this concept, is that of *ʿadam al-tasāmuḥ*.[71]

taʿaṣṣub (fanaticism). The modern use of this term represents a semantic extension. In earlier usage it

67. Maḥfūẓ, *Qaṣr al-Shawq* (Cairo, 1957), p. 65.

68. Wadīʿ Filasṭīn reminds us, however, that already in 1929 the word *irtisāmāt* was used by Shakīb ʾArslān as denoting the same meaning as *inṭibāʿāt*. See *Majallat al-Majmaʿ al-ʿIlmī al-ʿArabī* 39, no. 3 (Damascus: July 1964): p. 502.

69. Fuʾād ʾIfrām al-Bustānī, *Al-Shaykh ʾIbrāhīm al-Yāzijī: Fī al-Lughah wa al-ʾAdab* (Beirut, 1952), pp. 33–34.

70. Ibid., pp. 33–34.

71. *Minutes*, 3:284.

was a synonym of the etymologically related term *ᶜaṣabīyah*. In modern Arabic, however, the latter came to mean "nervousness," whenever not used in a sociological context.

The criterion of mold-application did not enter into the etymological reasoning behind a neologism like *thawrah* (revolution). Here we have a case of semantic extension from the classical meaning of "excitement," which this word carried. Further root-meanings, like "to be disorderly," "to be enraged," contributed to the full semantic shaping of the word and concept of revolution. *Thawrah*, with its modern meaning, was already used towards the end of the nineteenth century. The first translators of the *Madrasat al-ᵓAlsun*, in the times of Muḥammad ᶜAlī, were using the Form V infinitive *taghayyur* instead,[72] and the dictionary of Bocthor, too, suggests other easily derivable *maṣdar* forms: *taghyīr, taqallub, inqilāb*, as well as *qawmah*. From the latter, Bocthor also derives the adjective and adjectival noun, *qawmī* (revolutionary).[73]

The diminutive form may be used in derivation as well. Thus, Ḥasan Ḥusayn Fahmī proposes *kuhayrab* for "electron."[74]

A broadly used approach to lexical neologizing is that of deriving adjectives and abstract nouns by means of the *nisbah* suffix.[75] Examples of this method are so numerous and so familiar that a small sampling should suffice for our present purpose:

shuyūᶜīyah (communism)
ishtirākīyah (socialism)
masraḥīyah (play: theatrical)

72. See Jamāl al-Dīn al-Shayyāl, *Taᵓrīkh al-Tarjamah wa al-Ḥarakah al-Thaqāfīyah fī ᶜAṣr Muḥammad ᶜAlī* (Cairo, 1951), pp. 221–22.

73. Bocthor, *Dictionnaire français-arabe*, p. 271.

74. Fahmī, *Al-Marjiᶜ* (Cairo, 1958), p. 50. Wehr, *Dictionary of Modern Arabic*, registers the positive form, *kahrab*, only.

75. A *nisbah*-noun must not be an abstraction, however. Thus *sukkarīyah* (sugar bowl) is a concrete noun. The otherwise abstract *masraḥīyah* (play), when it designates a book as an object, becomes concrete as well. For older examples of such derivations, see above, p. 8.

al-ᶜishrīnīyāt	(the twenties)[76]
ᵓasbaqīyah	(precedence, priority; seniority)[77]
ᶜuḍwī	(organic). This term, together with its derivatives *lāᶜuḍwī* or *ghayru ᶜuḍwī* (inorganic), may be used in the sciences, or may be broadly conceptualized for literary use, as in *wa ᵓidhā kānat al-lughah kāᵓinan ᶜuḍwīyan ḥayyan* (an organic being)[78]
wuṣūlī	(parvenu), as in the expression: *ka shuᶜūbi ᵓūrubbā al-wuṣūlīyah*[79]
hurūbī	(escapist), as in *Al-ᵓilḥād sahl, ḥall sahl hurūbī. . .* (Apostasy is easy, an easy, escapist solution . . .)[80]

To conclude our discussion of the category of direct derivation, we shall take notice of a phenomenon which very frequently accompanies the modern effort of *ishtiqāq*, particularly in the language of science and technology. Thus we observe that the modern Arabic lexicon sometimes suffers as much from a superabundance of synonymous terms as it does from the lack of new vocabulary. The uncoordinated effort of individuals and academies in producing modern terminology may accumulate many synonyms which then, in their totality, become unruly if not altogether useless in a language which aims at terminological precision. A good example in this regard is furnished by the profusion of synonyms for the technical term "brake." Muṣṭafā al-Shihābī counts at least eleven neologisms coined for this device: (1) *al-kammāḥah*, derived from *kamaḥa* (to pull in: a horse) and proposed by the Cairo Academy; (2) *al-mūqif* (in Iraq); (3) *māsik* and (4)

76. Thus it is used by Yūsuf al-Khāl in the journal *ᵓAdab* 2, no. 1 (Winter 1963): 12. In Egypt, however, *ᶜishrīnāt, thalāthīnāt,* and so on.

77. For example, *ᵓasbaqīyat al-ḥaḍārah al-ᵓūrubbīyah;* see ᶜAbd al-Muḥsin Ṭāhā Badr, *Taṭawwur al-Riwāyah al-ᶜArabīyah al-Ḥadīthah fī Miṣr* (1870–1938) (Cairo, 1963), p. 35.

78. As used by Yūsuf al-Khāl, *ᵓAdab* 2, no. 1:8.

79. ᶜAbd al-Muḥsin Ṭāhā Badr, *Taṭawwur al-Riwāyah*, p. 385.

80. Najīb Maḥfūẓ: *Al-Sukkarīyah* (Cairo, 1958), p. 127. The word *hurūbī* does not yet figure in dictionaries of modern Arabic.

mikbaḥ (in Syria), the latter derived from *kabaḥa* (to check: a horse); (5) *al-lijām* (in the French-Arabic dictionary of al-Najjārī); (6) *al-ḥakamah* (in J. B. Belot's *Dictionnaire français-arabe*); (7) *al-ḍābiṭah* and (8) *al-kābiḥah* (in the English-Arabic Dictionary by A. Elias); (9) al-*mīqaf* (in a technical book); (10) *al-farmalah* (a colloquialism registered also by the Cairo Academy); (11) *al-firān* (a Syrian colloquialism).[81]

Derivation through approximation of older vocabulary to new meanings

This group consists of neologisms which are either figurative semantic extensions (*al-waḍᶜ bi al-majāz*), or reclaimed archaisms, only loosely related to the modern meanings (*gharīb al-lughah*).

The metaphoric method of derivation reveals the operativeness in Arabic of etymology outside of the formal root-derivation. In fact, it is not even a modern approach, since much of the early classical Arabic terminology in theology, philology, and the sciences owes its existence to this method. The modern contribution to it is only one of definition and of systematic analogical application.

While discussing the method of formal root-derivation, we have already called attention to some cases where a metaphoric etymology is apparent. In other instances only a situation of ambiguity can be detected, namely, a simultaneous awareness of the formal root-derivation as well as of semantic extension. At present we shall review the modern Arabic attitudes with respect to the method under consideration only.

Most of the new terms which have been obtained through metaphoric extension do not come from normative institutions like the academies. Here, as in most other respects, the translators, the journalists, the writers, and even the poets have been coining such derived terms for their own needs long before the academies had given them official sanction. Thus among the most current modern vocabulary we find examples of metaphoric extension:

81. See *Majmaᶜ al-Lughah al-ᶜArabīyah—Majmūᶜat al-Buḥūth wa al-Muḥāḍarāt* (1959–1960) 1:70.

ʾadab	(literature)[82]
jarīdah	(newspaper)[83]
majallah	(review, journal)[84]
bīʾah	(environment, milieu)[85]
qiṭār	(train)[86]

The translator of the *Iliad,* Sulaymān al-Bustānī (1856–1925), figures among the most consistent users of this method. To him Arabic literary terminology owes such neologisms as *malḥamah* (epos)[87] or *qaṣaṣī* (epic), but he also used the etymologically revealing compound *shiʿr al-malāḥim*. His coining of the Arabic equivalent for "lyrical" was less fortunate, since his term *mūsīqī* became superseded by the more recent *ghināʾī.*[88]

To the broad category of semantic extension which by means of abstraction opens up a word to unlimited possi-

82. There is no need for a complete discussion of the semantic and conceptual changes which this term has undergone, since there are appropriate reference materials in this respect: *The Encyclopaedia of Islam,* for example, or *Majmaʿ al-Lughah al-ʿArabīyah—Majmūʿat al-Buḥūth wa al-Muḥāḍarāt* (Cairo, 1960), 2:14–16.

83. This term, made current by ʾAḥmad Fāris al-Shidyāq (1805–1887), is a metaphoric derivation from the old meaning of "stripped palm-branch," used for inscriptions. See ʾAdīb Murūwah, *Al-Ṣiḥāfah al-ʿArabīyah* (Beirut, 1961), p. 14.

84. This term was introduced by ʾIbrāhīm al-Yāzijī as an extension of the classical: "book" (containing science), "writing." See Fuʾād al-Bustānī, *ʾIbrāhīm al-Yāzijī,* p. 35.

85. This neologism is due to ʾIbrāhīm al-Yāzijī, who also uses the adjective *bīʾī* (environmental). See ibid., p. 35. In the classical usage *bīʾah* refers to the mode of taking for oneself a place of abode, or to a certain kind of abode, or to a state.

86. This term gained an early and rapid acceptance. Linguistically it is one of the most perfect examples of etymology operating on different levels. Its classical meaning of a "file of camels" provides the visual analogy between an extended camel caravan and a file of railroad cars. At the same time the synonymity of "file" and "train" makes of it a translation of the term "train" in its many European versions. A further derivation from the root *qaṭara* provides also the term for "locomotive" (*qāṭirah*). It is interesting to observe how the Cairo Academy tried to maintain the metaphor of the camel caravan by proposing the word *hādiyah* instead of *qāṭirah* (*Minutes,* 2:166).

87. Sulaymān al-Bustānī, *ʾIlyādhat Hūmīrūs* (Cairo, 1904), p. 163.

88. He prided himself on being the first one to use this term. See above, footnote 87.

bilities of usage belong such words as *basāṭah* (simplicity), *basīṭ* (simple),[89] or *buᶜd* (dimension), as in *al-buᶜd al-ijtimāᶜī* (the social dimension)[90] and *kaᵓanna al-ᵓusṭūrata . . . qad iktasabat . . . buᶜdan thālithan ᵓaw rābiᶜan* (third or fourth dimension).[91] This group of derivatives, however, will be discussed in more detail separately.

In its effort to define the various forms of word-derivation, the Royal Academy of the Arabic Language in Cairo approached metaphoric extension as a useful way to provide new vocabulary for general as well as scientific use, particularly in cases where formal root-derivation was difficult to apply, or where regional colloquial and borrowed foreign terminology were sought to be replaced by terms obeying the classical word-molds. According to one view expressed within the Academy, new meanings should be given to archaic vocabulary (*gharīb al-lughah*) preferably, because such an approach would check the further increase of the already unruly wealth of the Arabic lexicon. If new terms are derived from archaisms only, the lexicon as such will not suffer, only its semantic content will shift. New meanings, however, should not be attached to those classical words which are still in use, because this would only aggravate the already serious problem of lexical ambiguity. Another condition insisted upon by the academicians was that the new meanings be to some extent related to the meanings of the basic roots of the built-upon classical words. This dependence upon root-meanings, however, was rarely maintained even by the academic neologizers themselves, and a broader concept of purely figurative similarity between the old and the new meanings prevailed. It is interesting that the views of the western members of the Academy were more reserved and cautious regarding the modern semantic use of classical vocabulary. To them such a borrowing of old words would necessarily mean a

89. See ᵓIbrāhīm al-Sāmarrāᵓī's remarks concerning the use of these words by the poet ᵓAḥmad al-Ṣāfī al-Najafī, in the former's *Lughat al-Shiᶜr* (Beirut, n.d.), p. 94.

90. *Ḥiwār* (Review) 3, no. 3 (March–April, 1965): 49.

91. ᶜAbd al-Muḥsin Ṭāhā Badr, *Taṭawwur al-Riwāyah*, p. 379.

depauperization of the Arabic language in its literary function.[92]

A theoretical position like that of the Cairo Academy, however, even though serving as a confirmation of an already existing process, failed to have an immediate effect upon the neologizing movement. Many words obtained by this method did not gain literary or scientific acceptance. Some, like the term *ʾirzīz*, whose old meaning is "sound of rain, of thunder" or "tremor," and to which the academician ʾAḥmad ʿAlī al-ʾIskandarī gave the modern meaning of "telephone," even became proverbial objects of ridicule. An eloquent example of the fruitlessness of the practical linguistic effort on the academic level in this respect was the discussion over a concise literary term for "skyscraper," one that would replace the composite calque *nāṭiḥat al-saḥāb*. According to the ruling of the Cairo Academy, which established that a one-word term should be preferred to a compound one, three possible substitutes were suggested: the now archaic *ṭirbāl* (high portion of a wall, high building), *ʾuṭm* (fortress, lofty building), and the still current *ṣarḥ* (castle, tower, high structure). After an excessively lengthy discussion which lasted through several sessions, the first two of the above terms were rejected by reason of their being etymologically of non-Arabic origin. Finally, the Academy adopted *ṣarḥ* as denoting "skyscraper," with the recommendation that, temporarily, it go accompanied and explained by the already current *nāṭiḥat al-saḥāb*.[93] Today, however, the only literary use made of *ṣarḥ* with reference to a skyscraper is purely metaphoric in the poetic sense.

The academic attempt to replace the colloquially current foreign term *trām* (streetcar, tramway) by the archaism *jammāz* (swift-footed ass or camel) failed equally, so that finally the Cairo Academy itself was forced to tolerate the foreign word.[94]

The archaism *ʾatī* (conduit of water, rivulet), suggested

92. For the discussion of this topic on the floor of the Cairo Academy, see *Minutes*, 2:76, 77, 79, 142–43, 166–67.

93. Ibid., 2:30–34, 53.

94. Ibid., 3:399–402.

by the Cairo Academy as the term for "siphon,"[95] remains disregarded. Instead, the semicolloquial *shaffāṭah* has gained literary acceptance. In the same way the old word *kawthal* (stern, tiller) did not impose itself over the compound *ᶜajalat al-qiyādah* (steering wheel), although the classical meaning of *kawthal* is gradually being revived as well.

The archaism *qashwah* (basket for feminine grooming objects) was proposed by ᶜAbd al-Qādir al-Maghribī for the modern term of "boudoir dressing table," "toilet."[96]

The word *ᶜajalah* (a wheeled cart or carriage; waterwheel) has experienced several modern semantic changes and thus became the standard term for "wheel." It also came to mean "bicycle." It entered into such composites as *al-ᶜajalah al-sayyārah* and *al-ᶜajalah al-nārīyah* (motorcycle). At the same time, another early word, *darrājah* (a wheeled support for an old man or a child), became figuratively extended to mean "bicycle," entering then into the composite *darrājah nārīyah* (motorcycle). The Cairo Academy's attempt to give the meaning of "motorcycle" to the classical word *zafzāfah* (a violent wind producing a continuous sound, similar to the onomatopoeic value of *zafzafa*), failed.[97]

Several other successful figurative extensions may be cited: *khalīyah* (cell), derived from the classical meaning of "beehive";[98] *ʾiḍbārah*, but also *ḍibārah* and *ḍubārah* (file,

95. Ibid., 1:448.

96. Ibid., 2:144. The term *qashwah* did not gain acceptance, however. The variously used word *tasrīḥah* (dressing table; hairdo, coiffure), used also in composites, has become the accepted term for this meaning. If one were to pursue al-Maghribī's approach, one could also suggest another classical word, *safaṭ* (basket or chest for beauty-articles of women), as an alternative to *qashwah*, although, it is true, the more archaic *qashwah* meets the Academy's position better.

97. *Majallat Majmaᶜ al-Lughah al-ᶜArabīyah al-Malakī* (Cairo, 1935), 1:122.

98. This term was already used in the early nineteenth century, according to ʾAḥmad ᶜAlī al-ʾIskandarī (*Minutes*, 2:248). The dictionary of Bocthor, however, contains only the words *khalal* as designating "cell," and *khalalī* for "cellular," both derived from the classical meaning "interstice," "interspace" (between walls). This

dossier), whose old meaning is "bundle" of books or writings; or the recent *ṣawmaᶜah* (silo), whose old meaning is that of "a monk's cell," but which is then also etymologically related to *ṣamᶜah* (wheat-bin) together with the verbal meaning of *ṣawmaᶜa* (to heap, to shape conically).[99]

Neologisms derived through translation or descriptive paraphrasis of foreign terms: al-ishtiqāq al-maᶜnawī—al-ishtiqāq bi al-tarjamah

Terms obtained by means of this method are very numerous. In spite of the classical Arabic tendency to coin one-word terms whenever possible, a tendency which in modern times has been at least formally recognized by the academies as well as by individual neologizers, the massive translation movement in the nineteenth century and the proliferation of journalism forced upon the modern Arabic language a flood of more or less rapidly coined compound words. As a rule these compound neologisms are the product of straight translations or "calques" of the models provided by European languages. Subsequent, more conventional attempts at reducing some of these composites to one-word terms have mostly failed. As a result, the composite Arabic word has now been fully sanctioned by linguistic habit. Very often, however, there exists a wide divergence—from one region to another or from one writer to the next—as to what composite neologism is to be preferred, since the paraphrastic nature of such derivations makes them particularly subject to the whims of individual taste.

The evolution of the term for "chamber of deputies" in Egypt may serve as an example of the various approaches which may be taken in the rendition of a complex term: *dīwān rusul al-ᶜamālāt,* as used by Rifāᶜah al-Ṭahṭāwī (1801–1873), is curiously precise in its inclusion of *ᶜamālāt* (districts, provinces), *majlis shūrā al-qawānīn* (legislative council), *al-jamᶜīyah al-ᶜumūmīyah* (general assembly),

---

similarity between *khalīyah* and *khalal* is not accidental, and reveals further etymological relationships.

99. *Al-ᵓAhrām* (6 April 1968), p. 1.

al-jamᶜīyah al-tashrīᶜīyah (legislative assembly), *majlis al-nuwwāb* (council, chamber of deputies), and so on.[100]

As can be seen above, these composite terms are translations of expressions, and therefore they could as well be included in that category (*taᶜrīb al-ˀasālīb*). As terms or semantic units, however, they have to be distinguished from the merely stylistic phenomenon of *taᶜrīb al-ˀasālīb*, to which separate attention will be given in due course.

Composite terms which have attained wide literary acceptance are, for instance: *markaz al-thiql* (center of gravity);[101] *markaz al-shurṭah* (police station), together with other composites containing *markaz; al-riwāyah al-istiᶜrāḍīyah* (revue);[102] or *takyīf al-hawāˀ* (air conditioning). These examples represent the simplest form of *al-ishtiqāq bi al-tarjamah.* The derivation through paraphrasis of concepts (*al-ishtiqāq al-maᶜnawī*) is best illustrated by the rendering into Arabic of the word "ideal" as *al-mathal al-ˀaᶜlā.*[103]

Many composite Arabic terms have variants or are not sufficiently current in their literary usage. This deprives them of the desirable semantic precision. Authors who use such terms tend to add to the Arabic version the original foreign form. The following examples can be considered as representative of this group.

The term "conditional reflex" is translated into Arabic sometimes as *al-inᶜikās al-sharṭī* and sometimes as *al-inᶜikās al-ẓarfī;*[104] "universality" is rendered either as

100. See a fuller list of these terms in Jamāl al-Dīn al-Shayyāl, *Taˀrīkh al-Tarjamah* (Cairo, 1951), p. 214.

101. Notice the abstract use of this term in "*markaz al-thiql al-ˀadabī al-siyāsī,*" *Al-ˀAbḥāth* 15, no. 3 (September 1963):337.

102. Notice Tawfīq al-Ḥakīm's use of *al-riwāyah al-istᶜrāḍīyah al-ᶜuẓmā* with the Calderonian meaning of *el gran teatro del mundo*, in *Qiṣaṣ Tawfīq al-Ḥakīm* (Cairo, 1949), 2:13.

103. ˀAḥmad ˀAmīn who, in his *Fajr al-ˀIslām* (7th ed., pp. 37–38), mentions *al-mathal al-ˀaᶜlā* as being a neologism and a concept originally nonexistent in Arabic is contradicted by ᶜUmar al-Dusūqī, who quotes the koranic verse "li al-ladhīna lā yuˀminūna bi al-ˀākhirati mathalu al-sūˀi wa li al-Lāhi al-mathalu al-ˀaᶜlā" (Sura XVI, 61) (*Fī al-ˀAdab al-Ḥadīth*, 3d ed. [Cairo, 1954], 1:330).

104. For the discussion of these two terms, see: *Apollo* 2, no. 3:194.

al-ʿumūmīyah al-sāmiyah or simply as *ʿumūmīyah;*[105] "humane" as *al-ʾinsānī al-ʿālī;*[106] "artificial breathing" as *al-tanaffus al-ṣināʿī;* "crossword puzzle" as *al-muʿammayāt al-ʾufqīyah al-raʾsīyah.*[107]

Using such composite terms, the Egyptian literary critic Muḥammad Mandūr, for example, almost always adds the original term behind the Arabic version. Thus we read *wahm al-ḥaqīqah*—"l'illusion du réel";[108] again, in the same book, he expresses the identical concept as *mushākalat al-wāqiʿ;*[109] *al-ʾīmān bi jamāl al-ṣiyāghah wa al-shakl*—"le culte de la forme";[110] *sarāb ʿāṭifī*—"pathetic fallacy";[111] *al-ruʾyah al-shiʿrīyah*—"vision poetique";[112] *ḥuzn khafīf*—"melancholie";[113] *ʿuṣūr al-dhawq*—"les epoques du goût."[114]

These last examples are extracted from a few pages of only a single book, so as to illustrate an important problem which confronts the modern Arab writer and which very often determines his style beyond the point of mere lexical innovation. The problem is that of participating in several other cultures besides one's own and of the impact of different foreign tongues upon one's capacity for and style of expression. A writer who is limited exclusively to the cultural scope of the Arabic language is more likely to write in an unadulterated language, because he thinks exclusively in Arabic and his thought is undisturbed—but also uninspired—by foreign associations. A writer of multiple cultures is exposed to inevitable and often dangerous conflicts of ideas in their literary conception and expression. Therefore it is only natural that there should be a difference of style between a writer of a homogeneous cultural background and one of a heterogeneous and cosmopolitan background.

In the literature of the *Nahḍah,* where the differences between old and new, self-contained and multicultural, are still very clearly discernible, this difference can be very strongly sensed. There are purists with no problems, with

105. Ibid., no. 6:441.
106. Ibid., no. 3:205.
107. Ibid. 1, no. 10:1198.
108. Muḥammad Mandūr, *Fī al-Mīzān al-Jadīd* (Cairo, 1944), p. 12.
109. Ibid., p. 35.
110. Ibid., p. 43.
111. Ibid., p. 72.
112. Ibid.
113. Ibid., p. 74.
114. Ibid., p. 134.

security of style and semantic uniformity, but with great limitations of means; and there are those who fill their pages with thought-provoking new material, but whose language is tortured by neologisms of their own making—words which are often altogether arbitrary and without any broad recognition. Sometimes these modern writers will strain the Arabic language beyond its point of tolerance, and this will entail a disharmony between concept and term, depriving words of their literary effectiveness. Where in the West the continuous use of concepts and terms throughout a prolonged period of intense literary life has imbued such terms with meaning and enriched their field of associations, in the young culture of the *Nahḍah* the process of conceptual impregnation and semantic precision has not yet reached a completely satisfactory level. Arab writers who explore untrodden paths of semantic experimentation and innovation all too often must recur to well-defined terms in other languages, in the form of fastidiously scholastic authoritative references. These references are disruptive not only of the formal purity of the language, but also of the natural train of thought.

In our discussion of composite neologisms, examples have been drawn, rather, from literary sources. There remains to be added that it is particularly in the modern Arabic language of science and technology that such neologisms gain the widest currency.

The derived verb

Verbal neologisms in modern literary Arabic, if compared with the nominal ones, are few in number and formal diversity. Totally new verbal roots are almost nonexistent, unless one takes into account the scarce number of purely colloquial verbal roots or the even rarer verbs of foreign origin which in their arabicized form have gained some—mostly local—acceptance.[115]

115. Thus the colloquial Egyptian arabicized verb *garraj* (to put in a garage); or the equally colloquial borrowing, although given literary respectability by Rifāᶜah al-Ṭahṭāwī, *kartana* (to put in quarantine). See his *Takhlīṣ al-ᵓIbrīz fī Talkhīṣ Bārīz* (Cairo, n.d.), p. 97.

As a result, verbal neologisms occur either in the derived verbal forms—in cases where such forms had not been used in classical Arabic—or as semantic extensions of already existing older verbal meanings.

New verbal derivatives may also be obtained from concrete nouns, either through primary derivation (*kahraba*, "to electrify"; ʾ*aqlama*, "to acclimate"), or through secondary derivation (*tamarkaza*, "to concentrate").

As regards the use of the verbal molds as the basis of derivation by analogy, the structure of the Arabic verbal system provides a sufficiently rigorous and transparent scale of so-called derived forms, with their inherent semantic connotations, to assist the Arabic linguistic sense in the application of the method of analogy. The analogical approach to verbal derivation in Arabic can, therefore, be considered a linguistic habit rather than a philological norm. Consequently, when the Royal Academy of the Arabic Language in Cairo concerned itself with the definition of the uses of the Arabic verbal forms, its discussions were conducted on a purely theoretical level and, as it were, as a matter of procedure only, without any substantial attempt to contribute actively to the practical effort of shaping verbal neologisms.[116]

Before turning to actual examples of modern verbal derivations, another general observation has to be made, namely, that the bulk of the modern Arabic verbal lexicon consists not of formal derivations of totally new words, but of semantically extended preexisting ones. The process of such semantic extension has affected a very high percentage of the classical verbal lexicon, indeed too high to allow a fuller treatment of this problem within the present chapter. The specific aspect of semantic extension, however, will be discussed in a separate chapter dealing with the phenomenon of semantic abstraction. Otherwise, only lexicography can do full justice to the modern semantic developments within the Arabic verb.

116. *Majallat Majmaᶜ al-Lughah al-ᶜArabīyah al-Malakī* (Cairo, 1935), 1:222–32.

One of the most frequent forms to be employed in modern verb derivations is Form II (*faᶜᶜala*). Thus, for example, *ṣawwata* came to mean "to vote." Although formally a semantic extension of the preexisting meaning of "to emit a sound, a voice," it should rather be considered as a denominative verb derivation from the term *ṣawt* (vote), which is the primary nominal semantic extension upon which the verbal derivation is based.[117]

The verb *maththala* is equally old in its diverse usages, except for the modern meaning of "to represent" pictorially, dramatically, and the like. As such it is a new semantic extension, obtained under the influence of analogy with similar semantic ramifications of its French and English equivalents.[118]

Only a remote connection exists between the modern meaning of the verb *sallaṭa* (to load, to charge with electric current) and the classical one (to give power, authority; to make prevail). Here the modern semantic extension is based on the modern synonymity between "power" and "electricity."

The verb *ḥallala*, in its modern meaning of "to analyze," may be considered a completely new derivation, formally as well as semantically. The classical meaning of the same word (to exculpate, to expiate, as by an oath) lacks in this case any practical etymological relevance. The modern verb *ḥallala* was obtained by means of an emphatic derivation from Form I, and acquired the meanings of "loosening," "breaking up," "dissolving," "diluting." Particularly from the last meaning, there was derived the meaning of "to analyze," as applicable in chemistry. A process of semantic extension and generalization then produced the present meaning, which is applicable to chemistry, psychology, literary criticism, and the like.

The verb *ṭawwara* (to develop) is a formal and semantic

117. See the Cairo Academy's discussion concerning this neologism in *Minutes*, 1:36–38.

118. The validity of this verbal derivation was debated on the floor of the Cairo Academy. Particularly questioned was its meaning which corresponds to the classical Arabic *nāba ᶜan*. . . . See ibid., pp. 41–43.

neologism.[119] It was derived analogically from Form V, under which form we shall further discuss its etymology.

Further instances of Form II neologisms are *kayyafa* (to condition), *shakhkhaṣa* (to personify, represent), *laqqaḥa* (to inoculate, vaccinate).

Modern verbal derivations of Form III are frequent, too. They suggest an action where mutuality is implied or anticipated. Most verbs which convey the meaning of addressing oneself to someone will have some degree of modern semantic extension or adaptation within this form, such as *rāsala, khāṭaba, khābara*, and the like. An interesting, completely new derivative within this group is the word *hātafa* (to telephone someone). It was proposed by Wadīᶜ Filasṭīn, as based on the nominal neologism *hātif* (telephone).[120]

The effect of analogy is particularly clear in the new derivative *jānafa* (to deviate from), as in the expression *wa lā nujānifu al-ḥaqīqata ḥīna naqūlu.*[121] To convey this meaning, classical Arabic uses only Form VI of this root (*tajānafa ᶜan*). In modern Arabic the free and natural use of *qiyās* allows this semantically unequivocal change to the transitive form.

In the case of *nāghama* (to hum softly to) we have a modern revival of a rare classical word. The vitality of modern analogical derivation may have reinstated this word without any awareness by modern writers of the existence of a classical antecedent.[122]

In some of its semantic extensions, the verb *wāᶜada* is

119. The verb *ṭawwara* is recent and relatively unfrequent in high literary usage. In the most recent journalism, however, it occurs much more frequently.

120. *Majallat al-Majmaᶜ al-ᶜIlmī al-ᶜArabī* 39, no. 3 (Damascus: July 1964):501.

121. Used by Sāmī al-Kīlānī in ibid., p. 433.

122. ᵓIbrāhīm al-Sāmarrāᵓī (*Lughat al-Shiᶜr*, p. 189) thinks erroneously that this form, as used by the poetess Nāzik al-Malāᵓikah, constitutes a new derivation. See, however, al-Zamakhsharī, *ᵓAsās al-Balāghah* (Cairo, 1960), and al-Tibrīzī in his commentary on the *Ḥamāsah* in Georg Wilhelm Freytag, *Hamasae carmina* (Bonn, 1847–51), p. 233.

a neologism too; thus, "to arrange for a rendezvous," "to date."[123]

Form IV verbal neologisms, although very numerous, fall almost invariably into the category of semantic extensions or derivations from already existing units. The modern semantic shift which takes place in such verbs does not necessarily obliterate the older meanings.

Thus, *ʾaḍraba* (*ʿan*), retaining its original meaning of "to leave," "to forsake," has also come to mean "to strike, to stop work"; *ʾakhraja*, together with a long list of older and newer meanings, can now be used as "to direct" a play, a film; *ʾantaja*, originally "to bear," "to throw," "to be near bearing," but also "to produce a result," has now acquired as its primary meaning that of "to produce," "to yield," as in industry; *ʾakhṭara* tends to lose most of its old meanings, acquiring instead the new ones of "to notify," "to inform," "to warn."[124]

The Form V verb in modern Arabic is, as a rule, very clearly defined as regards its inherent connotation, particularly in its reflexive relationship to the transitive Form II. Sometimes, however, in a given root a Form II verb may not even exist, as is the case with abstract verbs, or it may itself be derived from an already current Form V verb.

Thus, in its modern meaning, the verb *taḥammasa* (to be ardent, enthusiastic) is neither a derivation of a Form II verb, nor is it a direct semantic extension of the classical verbal meaning of "to behave with forced hardness or rigor." It owes its meaning, rather, to the also modern, but classically based, semantic development of the noun

123. See some examples of modern expressions containing Form III as well as Form VI of *waʿada* in: *Majallat al-Majmaʿ al-ʿIlmī al-ʿArabī* 39, no. 3 (Damascus: July 1964):502.

124. Sometimes a Form IV verbal derivation is used instead of another form, without thereby adding anything to the meaning. Such a purely formal variant is *ʾasfara bayna* (to serve as an intermediary) —instead of *safara bayna*—as in the following sentence by Najīb Maḥfūẓ: *liʾannahu huwa al-lādhī ʾasfara baynahu wa bayna ʾUmm Ḥamīdah* (*Zuqāq al-Midaqq*, 2d ed. [Cairo, 1955], p. 107).

ḥamāsah, as the latter acquired the meaning of "enthusiasm."[125]

The verb *taṭawwara* (to develop) is an example of a Form V derivative which made possible a more recent Form II derivative (*ṭawwara*). Formally, *taṭawwara* does not constitute a modern derivation. According to Muṣṭafā Jawād, it was already used by ᵓAbū Ḥayyān al-Tawḥīdī (died A.H. 414) and later, among others, by Ibn Khaldūn. The verb's original meaning was that of "to disguise oneself."[126] As such it appears to have been derived from the noun *ṭawr* (time, synonym of *tārah;* state, condition, manner). The present meaning of "to develop"—as to change from state to state—is only a modern semantic extension, with the Form II *ṭawwara* constituting a fully newly-derived verb.

The classical Form II verb *sammara* (to nail, to make firm) gave in modern Arabic the derivative *tasammara* (to be nailed down; but also, to stand as if nailed to the ground).

The very frequently occurring verb *takhayyala* (to imagine, fancy), in its "effective," transitive usage, has been considered by some modern philologists to be a misused neologism. This is not the case, however, since such a use of *takhayyala* was fairly common in prose from A.H. 300 on. It also occurs in the poetry of al-Ṣanawbarī (died A.H. 334).[127] Concerning this verb, one can therefore say that it represents a widespread modern usage, with one specific meaning, of a word which in classical Arabic would have had a wider variety of meanings.

The poet Jubrān Khalīl Jubrān used the Form V deriva-

125. When used with prepositions, *taḥammasa* acquires further semantic connotations, as in the following expression: *taḥammasa li al-Mutanabbī ᵓaw ḍiddahu nafarun* (some were either enthusiastically for al-Mutanabbī or fanatically against him). See Mandūr, *Al-Naqd al-Manhajī*, p. 191.

126. See: R. Dozy, *Supplement aux dictionnaires arabes*, 2:66; *Majallat al-Majmaᶜ al-ᶜIlmī al-ᶜArabī* 28, no. 3 (Damascus, July 1953):502–3. See also Monteil, *L'arabe moderne*, p. 111, where only the *maṣdar* form is considered.

127. See the pertinent verse by al-Ṣanawbarī quoted by ᵓAbū al-ᶜAlāᵓ al-Maᶜarrī in his *Risālat al-Ghufrān* (Cairo, 1950), p. 26.

tive *taḥammama* as a synonym of *istaḥamma* (to bathe).[128] Although a sound analogical derivation not quite void of earlier precedent, particularly as regards the classical usage of Form II of the same root (*ḥammama*), this derivation was tarnished as arbitrary.[129]

The Iraqi poet Badr Shākir al-Sayyāb uses the derivative *tawajjafa* with the meaning of "to be agitated, troubled, in commotion," as a synonym of *wajafa*. Neither classical nor modern dictionaries register this form. Analogy, however, makes its use permissible and semantically clear.[130]

The verb *takawwara* (to become round, ball-shaped) should be considered a neologism, although it might go slightly further back than the nineteenth century. Yet it has gained full circulation in modern writings only.[131]

Form VI has given modern Arabic many derivatives, most of them providing the mutual-reflexive aspect to the corresponding Form III verbs, as discussed above. Such Form VI neologisms do not need to be illustrated separately, since they are self-understood on the basis of analogy.

Examples of neologisms which contain the *qiyās* idea of mutuality, but which otherwise do not presuppose or entail Form III verbs of the same roots, are: *taḍāmana* (to be jointly liable; to be solidary); and *tarāmaqa* (to glance to each other), as in the expression *wa naḥnu natarāmaqu fī dhuhūlin wa ṣamtin*.[132]

Verbs that do not, semantically, directly reveal the linguistic logic of analogy are *takhāyala* (to appear dimly, in shadowy outline)[133] and the increasingly current usage of

128. *Jubrān Khalīl Jubrān: Al-Majmūʿah al-Kāmilah li Muʾallafātihi* (Beirut, 1959), p. 353 (in the poem "Al-Mawākib").

129. See Mīkhāʾīl Nuʿaymah's ironical reference to such a criticism of Jubrān in *Al-Ghirbāl* (Cairo, 1957), pp. 80–81.

130. ʾIbrāhīm al-Sāmarrāʾī, in *Lughat al-Shiʿr*, p. 221, comments on this usage by al-Sayyāb.

131. The novelist Najīb Maḥfūẓ uses *takawwara* fairly regularly, as, for instance, in *Qaṣr al-Shawq*, p. 356.

132. Najīb Maḥfūẓ, *Mīrāmār* (Cairo, 1967), pp. 267, 271. Dictionaries of modern Arabic do not register this verb.

133. Najīb Maḥfūẓ uses it frequently. The many other meanings of this verb are classical or, at least, premodern.

tarāmā as "to be vast," "to extend into the distance."[134]

The reflexive Form VII has not given modern Arabic many entirely new derivatives. Most verbs of this form had already existed in classical Arabic as formal units. It is in the field of semantic ramification and abstract extension of usage that this form has been particularly yielding.

The verb *insaḥaba*, in its modern meanings of "to retreat," "to pull out," "to be applied to," shows a semantic development that is more disassociated from the root-meaning. Other such verbs are direct semantic extensions which allow an abstract use in addition to the concrete classical one. This is the case with *insajama* (to be harmonious, orderly); *indamaja* (to be fused, to fuse; to be absorbed), as in the expression *indamaja al-mumaththilu fī dawrihi* (the actor became absorbed in his role, lived his role); *inkhafaḍa* (to decrease, be diminished), as in *inkhafaḍa al-ʾintāj* (the production decreased); *inᶜakasa* (to be reflected).

The method of analogical derivation becomes less viable in Form VIII, due to the fluctuation of this form between transitivity and intransitivity, the active and the passive meanings; and also because classical usage had already so extensively availed itself of this verbal mold.

For examples of modern derivations within Form VIII—semantically rather than formally—we may consider *intaḥara* (to commit suicide); *intaᶜasha* (to be stimulated, invigorated, to revive), as in the expression *intaᶜasha al-iqtiṣād* (the economy revived); *ibtakara* (to be original);[135] *iᶜtamada* (only as "to sanction, authorize something; to give on credit; to apply, employ, use); *iqtaṣada* (to be

134. As in the expression so common in Najīb Maḥfūẓ, *wa tarāmā al-maydānu fī ghāyatin min al-ittisāᶜi* (*Al-Ṭarīq* [Cairo, 1964], p. 25). Classical Arabic knows for this verb the opposite meaning (to pile up). The modern meaning of "to extend far" seems to have developed from idiomatic expressions based on the noun *al-marmā* (range, reach, extent), such as *baᶜīdu al-marmā*, and others.

135. Note, however, the use of this verb by ᶜAbd al-Lāh Ibn al-Muᶜtazz (died A.H. 296) in his *Kitāb al-Badīᶜ* (London, 1935), p. 2: ". . . wa lam yabtakirhumā al-muḥdathūna."

economical, to economize). In classical usage the last verb only conveyed the notion of a moderate, balanced action or attitude.

The Form X neologisms are relatively numerous, although their originality may easily be overestimated. Under closer examination, verbs which might strike us as modern will more often than not reveal a very close dependence on their classical etymological source of the same form.

Thus, *istaᶜmara* (to colonize, as a place) constitutes only a displacement of the object with respect to the classical meaning: "to make someone inhabit, cultivate (a place)." The classical meaning of *istaghalla* is "to demand the yield (of land)"; the modern usage adds only a semantic extension and a sociological emphasis, obtaining the meaning of "to exploit." The verb *istaqāla* (root: *q y l*) has added to its classical meanings the new one of "to resign," as in *istaqāla min manṣibihi* (he resigned from his post, office).[136] The verb *istajwaba*, which in old usage has the same meaning as *istajāba*, becomes analogically more precise in modern Arabic, as it comes to mean "to interrogate, examine, question."

Aside from the possibilities of derivation provided by the standard verbal molds of the triliteral verb system, there remains the linguistically interesting, although limited, phenomenon of the quadriliteral verbal neologism, derived from a concrete noun consisting of four letters. Thus are obtained: *kabrata* (to coat with sulfur; to sulfurize; to vulcanize); *tabalwara* (to crystallize); *markaza* (to concentrate something) and *tamarkaza* (to concentrate); *ᶜalmana* (to laicize); *qawlaba* (to mold); *ᵓaqlama* (to acclimate) and *taᵓaqlama* (to become acclimatized).[137]

136. According to Hans Wehr (*Dictionary of Modern Arabic*), the root *q w l* has given an entirely new verb: *istaqāla* (to render, as a voice by radio). Thus far I have not been able to verify the practical existence of this derivative. Instead, I have come upon the verb *istaqwala*, with the analogically based meaning of "to ask to speak."

137. See the discussion of such derivatives in the journal *Al-Lisān al-ᶜArabī*, no. 2 (Rabat, January 1965), p. 8; see also Monteil, *L'arabe moderne*, p. 110.

2. METATHESIS (QALB)

Metathesis reflects, most of all, the formative, archaic stages of the language, but it is also relatively frequent in medieval Arabic, as well as in colloquialisms.

Its characteristic feature is the change of position of the root consonants and the retention of the original meaning. Thus, *jadhaba* (to draw, to attract) may give *jabadha; laṭama* (to slap)—*lamaṭa; zawj* (spouse)—*jawz;* and so on. The root *sh w b* (to mix), for example, may give a number of derivations, such as *wishb*—(pl.) *ᵓawshāb; wabash*—(pl.) *ᵓawbāsh;* and *bawsh*—(pl.) *ᵓawbāsh* (for *ᵓabwāsh*); all of them meaning "mob," "medley," "rabble."

The influence of this form of derivation upon the formation of modern terms is a minor one in comparison to the simple or "small" derivation.

3. ROOT-MODIFICATION (ᵓIBDĀL)

Externally, root-modification consists in the change within a word of one of the radicals. The basic meaning of the root is retained either wholly or partly. Thus, *naᶜaqa, nahaqa,* and *naqqa* share the meaning of "animal cry" and "croaking." *Thalama* and *thalaba* mean "to slander"; and so on. Under *qalb* we already saw the change of *laṭama* into *lamaṭa*. The *ᵓibdāl* affects this root too, producing *ladama* and *lakama*, all of them possessing the same basic meaning of "to beat."

Essentially, the *ᵓibdāl* introduces us into the philosophy of Arabic lexicology. It is of fundamental importance to the understanding of the Arabic lexical structure, because it shows us the deeper origin of a word. Tracing the root affiliations and permutations which constitute the *ᵓibdāl*, we see how the Arabic word is generally reduced to only two meaning-determining radicals, with the third (or the fourth one) providing emphasis, nuance, or link with another root.[138]

138. See ᵓAḥmad Fāris al-Shidyāq, *Sirr al-Liyāl fī al-Qalb wa al-ᵓIbdāl* (Istanbul, 1284 [1867]). Here the nineteenth-century philologist tries to establish the onomatopoeic theory of the origin of the Arabic language and its reduction to biradical roots.

In modern literary Arabic, nevertheless, the ʾ*ibdāl* has played the least important role. The verb ʾ*ashshara*, for instance, constitutes a quasi-ʾ*ibdāl*. It is derived from the root *sh w r* in its Form IV: ʾ*ashāra*. The preformative ʾ*a* was incorporated as a root-letter, while the middle *w* disappeared. Semantically, too, the original "to show," "to point out," can be recognized in the new "to annotate," "to put a visa upon."[139] There exists also the interesting discussion over the term *masraḥ* (theatre), which seems to be a case of ʾ*ibdāl* and of *qalb* as well, if we accept that its original derivation is not that of the root *s r ḥ*. Whatever the case may be, the initiator of the Arabic theatre, Mārūn Naqqāsh (1817–1855), used the term *marsaḥ*.[140] In Lebanon this term remained current until fairly recent times, and men like Yaʿqūb Ṣarrūf and Shakīb ʾArslān acknowledge its precedence over the variant *masraḥ*.[141] But, according to these authors, the original term used for theatre was *marzaḥ* (low, depressed ground or land). Of old, popular festivals in Lebanon used to be held on such depressed grounds, which served as arenas in which the participants exhibited their skills in arms, and the like. On the declivities around gathered the spectators. This, accordingly, was the original *marzaḥ*, which later, through the ʾ*ibdāl*, had become the *marsaḥ* used by Mārūn Naqqāsh. A further process of metathesis or *qalb* produced the present *masraḥ*. Otherwise, there remains the explanation that *masraḥ*, meaning "meadow," "pasture ground," is a semantically extended direct derivation from the root *s r ḥ*.

139. See its discussion by ʾIbrāhīm al-Yāzijī in his *Lughat al-Jarāʾid* (Cairo, 1319 [1901]), p. 53.

140. Mārūn Naqqāsh, ʾ*Arzat Lubnān* (Beirut, 1869).

141. Al-Maghribī, *Al-Ishtiqāq*, pp. 81, 124.

The Formation of Compound Words (*Al-Naḥt*)

2

AL-NAḤT provides a completely different form of lexical creation. As the very term suggests, it consists in the chiseling out or sculpturing of words. The most frequent form of *naḥt*, and the one accepted by classical philologists, is the formation of a single new word out of two different, otherwise unrelated, words which are conveniently shortened (*manḥūt*). Thus, "belonging to Dār al-ᶜUlūm" is expressed by the compound *al-darᶜamah*, with its adjective *darᶜamī*.[1] The mixed genre between theatre (*masraḥ*) and novel (*riwāyah*) may be given the term *al-masriwāyah*.[2] In the *naḥt* as in the *ishtiqāq*, the principle of analogy with original Arabic molds (*qawālib*) can be rightfully and successfully applied, thus assuring the continuity of the essential characteristics of the language.

Among the old exponents of the principle of *naḥt*, the most copiously quoted by modern philologists is ᵓAḥmad Ibn Fāris (died A.H. 395), author of the *Al-Ṣāḥibī*. His are

1. See Maḥmūd Taymūr, "ᵓAlfāẓ al-Ḥaḍārah" in *Majmūᶜat al-Buḥūth wa al-Muḥāḍarāt* (Cairo, 1960), p. 180.

2. Tawfīq al-Ḥakīm would thus define his book, entitled *Bank al-Qalaq* (Cairo, 1966); see *Al-ᵓUsbūᶜ al-ᶜArabī*, no. 382 (10 March 1966), p. 47.

also the binding definitions of this principle.[3] Other authorities who deal with this question are al-Thaᶜālibī (A.H. 350–429), author of the *Kitāb Fiqh al-Lughah wa Sirr al-ᶜArabīyah,* and Jalāl al-Dīn al-Suyūṭī (A.H. 849–911), author of *Al-Muzhir.*

In modern Arabic philology, the principle of *naḥt* ranks among the linguistic issues which have aroused most interest and earned most attention. Thus, aside from its treatment by the academies,[4] more or less exhaustive studies have been dedicated to it by Jurjī Zaydān,[5] ᶜAbd al-Qādir al-Maghribī,[6] Muṣṭafā Ṣādiq al-Rāfiᶜī,[7] Sāṭiᶜ al-Ḥuṣrī,[8] and ᵓIsmāᶜīl Maẓhar.[9]

Still, the acceptance of *naḥt* was not unanimous. Reviving a classical dispute, some modern Arabic philologists claimed that Arabic was the language of *ishtiqāq* alone and that, in spite of the classical evidence, the possibilities of *naḥt* are now exhausted, its time past, and "its door closed." The representative of this point of view was the Egyptian ᵓAḥmad ᶜAlī al-ᵓIskandarī.[10] On the other hand, defending *naḥt*'s present use, Sāṭiᶜ al-Ḥuṣrī maintains that, especially in our modern times, lexical expansion by this means has become of a most pressing nature.[11]

In the already frequently mentioned book, *Al-Ishtiqāq wa al-Taᶜrīb,* ᶜAbd al-Qādir al-Maghribī has a very informative chapter on *naḥt,* which he considers to be a form of *ishtiqāq.* He divides it into four classes: *al-naḥt al-fiᶜlī* (verbal), *al-naḥt al-waṣfī* (adjectival), *al-naḥt al-ismī* (nominal), and *al-naḥt al-nisbī* (adjectival of reference).

3. ᵓAḥmad Ibn Fāris, *Al-Ṣāḥibī,* p. 227.

4. See the *Minutes* and the *Majallah* of the Cairo Academy; see also the small but interesting list of scientific terms constructed by Muḥammad Ṣalāḥ al-Dīn al-Kawākibī in *Majallat al-Majmaᶜ al-ᶜIlmī al-ᶜArabī,* 39, no. 3 (Damascus: July 1964):507–9.

5. Jurjī Zaydān *Al-Falsafah al-Lughawīyah,* pp. 71–97 (1st ed. in 1886).

6. Al-Maghribī, *Al-Ishtiqāq,* pp. 13–16 (1st ed. in 1908).

7. Al-Rāfiᶜī, *Taᵓrīkh ᵓĀdāb al-ᶜArab,* 1:187–89 (1st ed. in 1911).

8. Al-Ḥuṣrī, *ᵓĀrāᵓ wa ᵓAḥādīth,* pp. 13–147. The chapter on *naḥt* first appeared independently, in 1928.

9. Maẓhar, *Tajdīd al-ᶜArabīyah,* pp. 14–55.

10. Maẓhar, *Tajdīd al-ᶜArabīyah,* p. 17.

11. Al-Ḥuṣrī, *ᵓĀrāᵓ wa ᵓAḥādīth,* p. 129.

As for *al-naḥt al-fiʿlī*, it consists in the formation of a multiradical (more than three) verb out of a group of words which might also be a short nominal or verbal sentence. Thus we have the verb *baʾbaʾa*, meaning to say *bi ʾabī ʾanta; jaʿfala*, meaning to say *juʿiltu fidāʾaka; sabḥala*, as to say *subḥān al-lāh; ḥawqala*, as *lā ḥawla wa lā quwwata ʾillā bi al-lāh; damʿaza*, instead of *ʾadāma al-lāhu ʿizzaka; samʿala*, for saying *wa al-salāmu ʿalaykum*. A frequently used *manḥūt* verb, not mentioned by al-Maghribī, is *fanqala*, meaning to say *fa ʾin qīla kadhā qīla kadhā*.

Al-naḥt al-waṣfī consists in the formation of adjectives (generally with an emphatic meaning) out of two words which would complement each other, providing the desired connotation or emphasis. Thus, *ḍibaṭr* (firm, strong-bodied; a lion agile in its movements) is composed of *ḍabaṭa* (to hold fast) and *ḍabara* (to leap); *ṣildim* (strong-hoofed) is composed of *ṣalada* (to be hard) and *ṣadama* (to strike against); *ṣahṣaliq* (vehement of voice) is composed of *ṣahala* (to neigh) and *ṣalaqa* (to utter a loud shout).

Al-naḥt al-ismī is the formation of a new noun out of two mutually complementing words, as in the case of *julmūd* (large stone, rock), composed of *jaluda* (to become hard, strong) and *jamada* (to congeal, become solid).

Al-naḥt al-nisbī expresses the relation of somebody or something to two different places, schools, and so forth. Tabaristan and Khwarizm give the adjective *ṭabarkhazī*. Someone belonging to the schools of al-Shāfiʿī and ʾAbū Ḥanīfah is a *shafʿantī;* the Ḥanafīyah and the Muʿtazilāh would give *ḥanfaltī*.[12]

Al-Maghribī's study of *naḥt* does not introduce any new element, however. It is merely a systematization of the traditional material. A more unorthodox approach to this subject is to be found in Jurjī Zaydān, who studies the in-

12. Al-Maghribī does not take upon himself the defense of precisely these forms. He only wishes to show the possibilities of derivation which exist in Arabic. See his *Al-Ishtiqāq*, pp. 14–15. A clear example of the awareness of the correctness of such *nisbah* compounds is provided by Samʿānī (*Kitāb al-ʾAnsāb*) while maintaining that the adjective of *Maʿarrat al-Nuʿmān* is not *maʿarrī* but *maʿarnamī* (See *Encyclopaedia of Islām*, under *Maʿarrah*).

fluence of *naḥt* upon colloquialisms of difficult etymology. He also tries to trace this principle to its simplest forms, such as the declension, the suffixes, prepositions, and the like.

With regard to the possibilities of *naḥt* in the present state of the language, however, the most interesting studies from the pragmatic point of view are those of Sāṭiᶜ al-Ḥuṣrī and ᵓIsmāᶜīl Maẓhar. Both recognize its applicability in the field of technical terminology. For ᵓIsmāᶜīl Maẓhar it is zoology and botany which are in the greatest need of adequate terminology, and an effective method to provide this terminology would be that of *naḥt*.[13] According to Maẓhar, the modern processes of *naḥt*-derivation should be analogical to classical philological patterns.[14]

Sāṭiᶜ al-Ḥuṣrī does not limit the modern application of *naḥt* to the language of the sciences. He thinks its need and usefulness are general. The particular originality of his contribution to the study of *naḥt* consists in his singling out and exploiting the possibilities in Arabic to form compound words by means of prefixes.

Thus, the negative particle *lā*, used as prefix, would make possible the creation of terms like: *lājtimāᶜī* (asocial); *lāᵓakhlāqī* (amoral); *lātanāẓurī* (asymmetrical); *lāmāᵓī* (anhydride); and the like.

Ghibba (after), used as prefix, would give terms like: *ghibmadrasī* (postscholarly); *ghibjalīdī* (postglacial); *ghibbulūgh* (postpuberty); and so on.

Qabla (before), if used as prefix, could give all those terms beginning with "pre . . .". Thus we should obtain: *qabtaᵓrīkh* (prehistory); *qabmanṭiqī* (prelogical); *qabbulūgh* (prepuberty); and so forth.

Further possibilities of this kind are those of using as prefixes short (*manḥūtah*) forms of *khārija—khāmadrasī* (extrascholarly); of *fawqa—fawsawī* (above-normal); and of *taḥta—taḥshuᶜūrī* (subconscious).[15]

These negative, temporal, and place prefix formations

13. Maẓhar, *Tajdīd al-ᶜArabīyah*, p. 17.

14. Ibid., pp. 72–73. See also the suggestions of Ḥasan Ḥusayn Fahmī, *Al-Marjiᶜ*, p. 41.

15. Al-Ḥuṣrī, *ᵓĀrāᵓ wa ᵓAḥādīth*, pp. 142–44.

suggested by Sāṭiᶜ al-Ḥuṣrī, are indeed capable of substantially enriching, and in many ways simplifying, modern Arabic vocabulary, but at the same time they are to be looked upon as essentially non-Arabic and non-Semitic, and as a characteristic feature of the Indo-European and the agglutinative languages.[16] Of course, this jeopardizes somewhat the principle of analogy with molds originally Arabic which, in theory, should be always binding and inflexible. Yet, even here there exists an historical argument in favor of the prefix. For prefix-groups or formations with the negative particle *lā* are not a complete novelty in Arabic. Sāṭiᶜ al-Ḥuṣrī lists as older Arabic forms such examples as *lāmutanāhī*, *lāḍarūrī*, *lādāʾimī*, *lāmawṣūfīyah*, and *lā-ʾadrīyah*.[17]

A full literary acceptance of such words, which would have implied their use in poetry, was as yet absent. But already in Abbasid poetry there can be detected the tendency towards using the group *lā shayʾ* as a lexical unit, as in this verse by ʾAbū Tammām:

ʾA fīya tanẓimu qawla al-zūri wa al-fanadi
wa ʾanta ʾanzaru min lā shayʾa fī al-ᶜadadi.[18]

And even when al-Mutanabbī, in the wake of ʾAbū Tammām, replaces *lā shayʾa* by *ghayru shayʾin*, he still pursues the effect of a single word-unit:

Wa ḍāqat al-ʾarḍu ḥattā kāda hāribuhum
ʾidhā raʾā ghayra shayʾin ẓannahu rajulā.[19]

16. Vincent Monteil suggests that Sāṭiᶜ al-Ḥuṣrī's predilection for *naḥt* and agglutination may be due to his Turkish origin (*L'arabe moderne*, p. 133). Yet it seems quite obvious that, in recurring to *naḥt*, Sāṭiᶜ al-Ḥuṣrī had European languages in mind.

17. See also Jurjī Zaydān, *Al-Lughah al-ᶜArabīyah Kāʾin Ḥayy*, rev. ed. (Cairo: Dār al-Hilāl, n.d.), p. 86; also Hans Wehr, *Die Besonderheiten des heutigen Hocharabischen* (Berlin, 1934), p. 37; and Monteil: *L'arabe moderne*, p. 138.

18. ᶜAlī ᶜAbd al-ᶜAzīz al-Jurjānī, *Al-Wasāṭah bayna al-Mutanabbī wa Khuṣūmihi*, 4th ed. (Cairo, 1966), p. 424. This is the *maṭlaᶜ* of ʾAbū Tammām's satire of Muḥammad Ibn Yazīd. The third verse of this poem contains the image imitated by al-Mutanabbī in the verse quoted below in the text.

19. ʾAbū Ṭayyib al-Mutanabbī, *Dīwān* (Beirut, 1964), 1:111.

As already noticed by Muḥammad Mandūr, this is a new type of language, borrowed from the philosophers.[20] Its use in poetry was not appreciated in ᵓAbū Tammām's and al-Mutanabbī's times.

In ᵓAbū Tammām *lā shayᵓa* is clearly only one word: a compound, a new linguistic usage, besides representing a new concept as well, and poeticizing it. When the initially morphologically rigid compound is submitted to full declension, Arabic "opens its door" to this specific kind of *naḥt*.

As regards the present linguistic and literary practice, the prefix form with *lā* has undoubtedly become generally accepted. What is more, it was widely used by modernists of the *Nahḍah* some time before Sāṭiᶜ al-Ḥuṣrī had published his essays, finding its way even into poetry.[21] In most cases the modern prefix formations with *lā* are still a shortened substitute for groups with *ghayr*. Yet, their capability of receiving the definite article makes them more flexible. Let us see here one example where *lā* and *ghayr* are actually interchangeable:

Min riḥlatin dhahabat ᵓilā lā rajᶜatin
ᵓaw furqatin rāḥat li ghayri talāqī.[22]

Still, we see that they are interchangeable only because both groups—*lā rajᶜatin* and *ghayri talāqī*—are indefinite.

Even more often, we encounter the group *ghayru ᶜawdatin* with a distinct character of intrinsic prefix formation. Thus, for example, ᵓAbū Shādī says: "Fa qad ᵓāna li mithli hādhihi al-munāqashāti wa dawāᶜīhā ᵓan tadhhaba ᵓilā ghayri ᶜawdatin."[23] Now, *ghayru ᶜawdatin* can be replaced by *lā ᶜawdatun* and used with normal noun declension (*ᵓiᶜrāb*), definite and indefinite.

Theoretically, the numerical possibilities of these formations should be unlimited, but in actual linguistic prac-

20. Mandūr, *Al-Naqd al-Manhajī*, p. 157.

21. Muḥammad ᶜAbd al-Munᶜim Khafājī, *Al-Shiᶜr wa al-Tajdīd* (Cairo, 1958), p. 398. The poet in question is Jamīl Ṣidqī al-Zahāwī.

22. Maḥmūd ᵓAbū al-Wafā, *Apollo* 2, no. 4 (December 1933), p. 335.

23. ᵓAḥmad Zakī ᵓAbū Shādī, *Apollo* 2, no. 4 (December 1933) p. 266.

tice their number is relatively small and mostly limited to abstractions. Hans Wehr includes in his dictionary the following ones: *lāʾibālīyah, lāʾadrīyah al-lāʾanāh, lājinsīyah, lādīnī, lādīnīyah, lāsāmī, lāsāmīyah lāsilkī, lāshuʿūr, lāshayʾ, lāshayʾīyah, lāmubālāh, lāmarkazīyah, lāmasʾūlīyah, lāniẓām, lānihāʾī, lānihāʾīyah.*[24]

The examples compiled by Hans Wehr do not exhaust this category. Other similar words frequently used are: *al-lātanāhi* (the infinite),[25] *al-lāwaʿy* (the unconsciousness),[26] *al-lāmaḥdūd* (the unlimited),[27] *lāḥaythu* (nowhere),[28] *al-lāmakān* (the nowhere),[29] *al-lāzamān* (the timelessness),[30] *al-lākiyān* (the nonbeing),[31] *al-lāʾamsi* (the nonyesterday),[32] *al-lāghad* (the nontomorrow),[33] *al-lābushr* (the hopelessness),[34] *al-lāʿurūbah* (the antiarabism),[35] *lāʾirādī* (involuntary),[36] *lāsabab* (nonreason),[37] and so forth.

On the whole, it is interesting and indicative to note that these prefix innovations should have found an early and predominant acceptance among Lebanese and Syrian writers and, in a particular way, among the poets of the American *mahjar*. In Egypt, on the other hand, they remained extremely rare, and only in the last two decades

24. Hans Wehr, *Dictionary of Modern Arabic.*

25. See above, n. 21, on Jamīl Ṣidqī al-Zahāwī; see also ʾIbrāhīm al-ʿUrayyiḍ, *Min al-Shiʿr al-Ḥadīth* (Beirut, 1958), p. 231 (the poem in question is "Wa ʾanā waḥdī maʿa al-layl," by Fadwā Ṭūqān).

26. ʾAnīs al-Khūrī al-Maqdisī, *Al-Ittijāhāt al-ʾAdabīyah fī al-ʿĀlam al-ʿArabī al-Ḥadīth* (Beirut, 1960), pp. 403, 409.

27. ʾIḥsān ʿAbbās, Muḥammad Yūsuf Najm, *Al-Shiʿr al-ʿArabī fī al-Mahjar* (Beirut, 1957), p. 42; see also *Apollo* 2, no. 5:378.

28. See the poem "ʾIlā al-Shāṭiʾ al-Majhūl" by Sayyid Quṭb.

29. As used in poetry by Nāzik al-Malāʾikah; see ʾIbrāhīm al-Sāmarrāʾī, *Lughat al-Shiʿr*, p. 168.

30. ʾIbrāhīm al-Sāmarrāʾī, *Lughat al-Shiʿr*, p. 168.

31. Ibid., p. 184.

32. Ibid.

33. Ibid.

34. Ibid., p. 195.

35. Yūsuf al-Khāl in *ʾAdab* 2, no. 1 (Winter 1963):10.

36. Najīb Maḥfūẓ, *Al-Sukkarīyah*, p. 134.

37. Yūsuf ʾIdrīs, *Lughat al-ʾĀy-ʾāy* (Cairo, 1965), p. 73. Compare his ". . . li lāsababin maʿqūlin ʾaw ghayri maʿqūlin," with the correct classical usage, as in al-Jāḥiẓ: "Wa al-ḥirṣu lā ḥadda lahu wa lā nihāyata li ʾannahu saʿyun *lā li ḥājatin.*" See al-Jāḥiẓ, *Rasāʾil al-Jāḥiẓ* (Cairo, 1964), 1:156.

did Egyptian writers really incorporate them into the current literary language. The contemporary generation of Iraqi poets, too, displays a definite predilection for the *lā* prefix.

Aside from the increasing modern tolerance of prefix word-units in the orthographic sense, there is also an awareness of the possibility of quasi-prefix formations, which in English would correspond to words prefixed by means of a dash. Through this method ʾAbd al-Ṣabūr Shāhīn obtains terms like: *bayna ʾasnānī* (inter-dental), *wasṭa ḥanakī* (mid-palatal), *ʾaqṣā ḥanakī* (post-palatal).[38]

38. See Henri Fleisch (al-ʾAb Hanrī Flaysh al-Yasūʿī), *Al-ʿArabīyah al-Fuṣḥā: Naḥwa Bināʾin Lughawīyin Jadīdin* (Beirut, 1966), p. 17. The book is a translation from the French, done by ʿAbd al-Ṣabūr Shāhīn and provided by him with an introduction in which he explains the method followed in obtaining Arabic terminological equivalents.

The Assimilation of Foreign Words (*Al-Taᶜrīb*)

3

ONE of the most important factors which contributed to the rapid modernization of the Arabic language was the assimilation of vocabulary of foreign origin. The technical term for this process is that of *taᶜrīb* (arabization). Yet *taᶜrīb*, as a solution to the urgent need for adequate modern terms in science, literature, and everyday life, was not unanimously accepted. Even though the translators of the school established by Muḥammad ᶜAlī of Egypt used foreign terminology with great profusion, it was clear almost from the very beginning that many of those crude neologisms were bound to disappear, and that *taᶜrīb* as such was not going to be the main source of the growth of the language. The challenger of *taᶜrīb* was, of course, *ishtiqāq*, which began gaining strength since the second half of the nineteenth century. Nevertheless, most of the men of the *Nahḍah* were wholly aware of the fact that total opposition to *taᶜrīb* would be unreasonable as well as impracticable, and in their methodological discussions they were largely concerned with the practical questions its application presented. Yet, besides such practical questions, there remained latent a more serious discrepancy of opinions, concerning the very nature of the arabicized words, their function and their place in the scale of values of the language. Out of such theoretical considerations there developed the opinion that the function of the arabicized neologisms had to be provisional only. These neologisms should be eliminated from the language in the same way as alien substances are eliminated from the organism, as soon as there were created or derived Arabic terms capable of replacing them. The hierarchical position and, consequently, the literary value of such provisional neologisms would be the lowest possible.

In opposition to this opinion the argument was raised that assimilation of foreign vocabulary is a process which has its roots in the very origins of the Arabic language, in some of its best poetry and even in the Koran. Assimilation, therefore, neither contaminates nor degrades the language, and arabicized words should be recognized and treated as permanent values.

The point of view adverse to *taʿrīb* is represented by Maḥmūd Shukrī al-ʾĀlūsī, ʾAḥmad ʿAlī al-ʾIskandarī, and Muṣṭafā Ṣādiq al-Rāfiʿī; that of its defenders, by Muḥammad al-Khuḍarī, ʿAbd al-Qādir al-Maghribī, ʾAḥmad Fatḥī Zaghlūl, Ṭaha Ḥusayn, and Yaʿqūb Ṣarrūf.[1]

The discussion of *taʿrīb* has a long history among Arab philologists. A recollection of this discussion may help us to define more precisely the methods pursued by the Arabs in the assimilation of foreign vocabulary—methods which have come down to the philologists of the *Nahḍah* strengthened by tradition and converted into binding rules.

The first philologist to become aware of foreign words in the Arabic language was apparently Ibn ʿAbbās (died A.H. 68), the cousin of the Prophet. His primary concern with the Koran led him to inquire into the etymologies of its vocabulary. As a result, there is attributed to him and to his school the singling out of a series of koranic words as being of foreign origin. Among these words are: *tannūr*,

1. See, for example, al-Maghribī, *Al-Ishtiqāq*, pp. 120–31, 148–50. See also Wehr, *Die Besonderheiten des heutigen Hocharabischen*, pp. 9–10.

ṭūr, yamm, rabbānīyūn, ṣirāṭ, qisṭās, firdaws, istabraq, and others.[2] In the following one hundred years, substantial progress was made in the tracing of foreign etymologies. Thus, the author of the *Kitāb al-ᶜAyn,* the famous al-Khalīl Ibn ᵓAḥmad (died A.H. 175), includes in his lexicon a number of these etymologies, and his disciple Sībawayh (died A.H. 180) dedicates several chapters of his grammar to this problem.[3] Further progress in discovering new foreign etymologies was made by ᵓAbū ᶜUbaydah (died A.H. 209), al-ᵓAṣmaᶜī (died A.H. 214), Ibn Qutaybah (died A.H. 276), Ibn Durayd (died A.H. 321), al-Jawharī (died A.H. 398), Ibn Sīdah (died A.H. 458), and al-Jawālīqī (A.H. 466–539), the author of a dictionary specifically dedicated to words of non-Arabic etymology, entitled *Al-Muᶜarrab.* Al-Jawālīqī's work collects the materials that other lexicographers before him had gathered, providing them with a critical review of his own.[4]

Not all of those early lexicographers and grammarians, however, shared identical views as to the nature of the arabicized words and as to the definition of *taᶜrīb.* Thus we see that, whereas Ibn ᶜAbbās had an unprejudiced approach to vocabulary of foreign origin, admitting its presence in the koranic text, later philologists, inspired by ᵓAbū ᶜUbaydah, tend to conceal that fact through hair-splitting sophisms.[5]

The most important differences of opinion, however, de-

2. A. Siddiqi, *Studien über die persischen Fremdwörter im klassischen Arabisch* (Göttingen, 1919), pp. 12–13. For more koranic vocabulary of non-Arabic origin see ᶜAbd al-Qādir al-Maghribī, *Al-Ishtiqāq,* pp. 27–29.

3. Sībawayh, *Kitāb Sībawayh,* ed. Derenbourg (Paris, 1881), 2:18–19, 208–9, 375–76.

4. For more information about *taᶜrīb* in old Arabic, mainly concerning the assimilation of Persian vocabulary, see Siddiqi, *Studien;* and Murād Kāmil, "Persian Words in Ancient Arabic," in *Bulletin of the Faculty of Arts* (Cairo University) 19, pt. 1:55–56.

5. ᵓAḥmad Ibn Fāris, *Al-Ṣāḥibī,* p. 29; and A. Siddiqi, *Studien,* pp. 13–14; see also, ᵓAnīs al-Khūrī al-Maqdisī, *Taṭawwur al-ᵓAsālīb al-Nathrīyah fī al-ᵓAdab al-ᶜArabī* (Beirut, 1935), 1:33–35, where the author recapitulates the old discussion around this problem, and also adds a list of the non-Arabic koranic vocabulary, extracted from the *Al-Muᶜarrab* of al-Jawālīqī.

veloped around the question of whether all the foreign words used by the Arabs should be considered as assimilated or *muʿarrabah*. Sībawayh, himself of non-Arabic origin, shows a rather lively interest in these problems. His definition of *taʿrīb* appears to be the most liberal one, and much of it will be rejected by later philologists. We shall quote it entirely, because, besides representing the position of a substantial school of classical grammarians and lexicographers, it stands closest to the present concept of *taʿrīb:*

> They [the Arabs] change those foreign words which are absolutely incongruous with their own, sometimes assimilating them into the structure of their words, and sometimes not. As for that which they assimilate into their forms, there is: *dirham*—according to *hijraʿ*; *bahraj*—according to *salhab; dīnār* as well as *dībāj*—according to *dīmās;* furthermore, they say *ʾIsḥāq*—according to *ʾiʿṣār; Yaʿqūb*—according to *yarbūʿ*; *jawrab*—according to *faʿwal;* and then they say *ʾājūr*—according to *ʿāqūl; shubāriq*—according to *ʿudhāqir; rustāq*—according to *qurṭās*.
>
> When they want to arabicize foreign words, they assimilate them into the structure of Arabic words in the same manner that they assimilate their letters to Arabic letters. Often they change the condition of a word from what it was in the foreign language, by assimilating to Arabic letters such as are not Arabic, and replacing a letter, even though it be like Arabic, by another one. Furthermore, they change the vocalization and the position of augmentative letters, without reaching by it the Arabic word structure, for, after all, it is a word of foreign origin whose power to attain the Arabic word structure is in their view not sufficient. To this they are impelled by the fact that the foreign words are changed by their incorporation into Arabic and alteration of their letters, and this change brings about the substituting and the changing of the vocalization, as the Arabs themselves do in the *nisbah*-construction when they say *hanī* according to *zabānī* and *thaqafī*.
>
> Frequently they shorten, as in the *nisbah*-construction, or they add, whereby they either attain the Arabic structure or not, as in the case of: *ʾājurr, ʾibrīsam, ʾIsmāʿīl, sarāwīl, fayrūz,* and *al-qahramān*.
>
> This they have done with both what was incor-

> porated into their word structure and what was not incorporated, in the way of change, substitution, addition and elision—all according to the change required.
>
> Often they leave a noun unchanged when its letters are like theirs—be its structure Arabic or not, as the cases of: *Khurāsān*, *ḥurram* and *al-kurkum*.
>
> Frequently they change a letter which does not exist in Arabic, without changing the original Persian structure of the word, as in *firind*, *baqqam*, *ʾājurr* and *jurbuz*.[6]

Of course, Sībawayh does recognize the trend and the tendency towards complete assimilation, but *taʿrīb* for him is a very broad concept. It comprises all the foreign vocabulary used by the Arabs, however distant from the original morphological molds of the Arabic language some of it might be.

A more rigid and discriminating approach to the assimilation of foreign vocabulary is that of the famous lexicographer al-Jawharī, author of the *Siḥāḥ*. Al-Jawharī's concern with the purity of the language demands a strict observance of the *qawālib*, for these alone can actually arabicize a foreign word. Otherwise it will always remain *ʾaʿjamī*. Al-Ḥarīrī maintains a similar point of view. According to him, "the Arabic criterion is that, whenever a foreign noun is arabicized, it is referred in type and form to similar Arabic words."[7]

As for the actual linguistic practice, it was the purists' criterion which prevailed over that of Sībawayh. Even though many foreign words entered the Arabic language, the number of words which do not adhere to the *qiyās* of the philological molds is insignificant. Among them are: *Khurāsān*, which would give the non-Arabic mold of *fuʿālān; ʾIbrāhīm* (*ʾifʿālīl*); *qunnabīṭ* (*fuʿʿalīl*); *ʾiṭrīfal*, *ʾihlīlaj*, and *ʾibrīsam* (*ʾifʿīlal*); *ʾājurr* (*fāʿull*); and *shaṭranj* (*faʿlall*).

The construction of derived forms from such foreign

6. *Sībawayh*, 2:375.

7. ʾAbū Muḥammad al-Qāsim Ibn ʿAlī al-Ḥarīrī, *Kitāb Durrat al-Ghawwāṣ fī ʾAwhām al-Khawāṣṣ* (Leipzig: Thorbecke, 1871), p. 131.

molds is generally considered as illicit, particularly by the school of al-Jawharī and al-Ḥarīrī.

In the period of Arabic cultural exhaustion and decadence which became accentuated after the Mongol invasion and continued through the centuries of Ottoman rule, the Arabic language was exposed to strong foreign influences, yet, within its strictly literary form, it was saved from irreversible contamination by its hermetic self-seclusion and inertia. Therefore, most of the vocabulary assimilated during that time without concern for the purity of the *qawālib* should be considered as extraliterary, if not starkly vernacular. The definitive lexicographical codification of the classical language which occurred precisely in those centuries reflects a strictly orthodox movement for preservation of the language.[8]

We have already seen how the modern attitudes to *taʿrīb* fall into two opposing camps. Among those with a positive approach to it, however, there is a significant division of opinion, which in its essence is but the reflection of the two antagonistic definitions of *taʿrīb* established by Sībawayh on one hand and al-Jawharī and al-Ḥarīrī on the other hand. Especially, the liberal definition of Sībawayh, which implies that everything used by Arabs is arabicized, has found eager acceptance in these urgent and feverish times of modernization. Thus, ʿAbd al-Qādir al-Maghribī writes in 1908:

> Our position with respect to *taʿrīb* is the reverse of that of the Arabs: whereas they seldom let a foreign word retain its original form, we would rarely change it in accordance with the patterns of our language. Thus, we pronounce telegraph, telephone, phonograph, automobile, theatre, program and many similar words, almost as they come down in their pronunciation, yet we term them as arabicized . . . in accordance with the method of the blessed Sībawayh.[9]

8. Ibn Manẓūr, the author of *Lisān al-ʿArab*, lived from A.H. 630 to 711 [A.D. 1232–1311]; al-Fīrūzābādī, the author of *Al-Qāmūs al-Muḥīṭ*, lived from A.H. 726 to 817 [A.D. 1326–1414]; and Murtaḍā al-Zabīdī, the author of *Tāj al-ʿArūs*, lived from A.H. 1146 to 1206 [A.D. 1732 to 1791].

9. Al-Maghribī, *Al-Ishtiqāq*, p. 43.

Although al-Maghribī himself is an ardent defender of *taᶜrīb*, he nevertheless harbors a certain reserve in respect to its definition by Sībawayh. Thus he continues:

> However much we approve of the point of view of Sībawayh in not regarding as a condition for the arabicisation of a word its assimilation according to the methods and molds of our language, it is necessary that in our indulgence we should stop at a certain limit. Otherwise, foreign words of different types and forms will multiply in our literary language to the extent that, with the passage of time, it might lose its character and become a hybrid language—neither Arabic nor foreign—something like the language of Malta or the remaining vernacular dialects of the different regions of Islamdom.[10]

As we have seen at the beginning of our discussion of *taᶜrīb*, the early translators lacked al-Maghribī's sense of moderation. But the flood of undigested foreign words which they were introducing was soon checked by the more powerful criterion of *ishtiqāq*. This criterion and the *qiyās* which lies at its base also influenced and shaped the further methods of loan-word assimilation. The philological conscience demanded from the new Arab writer some basic observance of the essential characteristics of his language. Yet, on the other hand, his increasing familiarity with foreign tongues was enabling him to introduce foreign words with much more phonetic and semantic precision and discipline than had ever been done in the past. Whereas the classical Arabic philologist and lexicographer was concerned with language only, and was faithful and loyal to it exclusively, his modern successor, even though sharing his love for Arabic, experienced an intellectual tension unknown in the past. He sometimes felt a divided loyalty and scientific remorse which prohibited him from mutilating foreign words in order to arabicize them. Another important reason why the more direct incorporation of foreign words maintains its position is the need for unequivocal clarity and precision in scientific terminology.

10. Ibid., pp. 43–44.

The school in modern *ta*ᶜ*rīb* similar to the old one represented by al-Jawharī demands a complete incorporation of all foreign elements into the Arabic lexicological system. This means that all neologisms should be molded and assimilated according to Arabic word-patterns. As a typical representative of this school we could consider the Iraqi poet and educator, Maᶜrūf al-Ruṣāfī.[11] In his efforts to include modern technological terms in Arabic poetry, he had necessarily to force them into the existing Arabic poetic metres. Thus, for example, instead of the usual form, *ᵓūtūmūbīl*, frequent in Arabic prose prior to the derived (*mushtaqq*) term, *sayyārah*, we find in his poetry:

Bi tūmubīlin jarā fī al-ᵓarḍi munsariḥan
kamā jarā al-māᵓu min safḥi al-ᵓahāḍībi.[12]

Similar conservatism and orthodoxy characterize the position taken with respect to *ta*ᶜ*rīb* by the Royal Academy of the Arabic Language in Cairo.[13]

A conciliatory approach to the problem of *ta*ᶜ*rīb* is that of Maḥmūd Taymūr. Even though he prefers, as most Arab writers do, the method of *ishtiqāq*, he would not reject *ta*ᶜ*rīb* completely. Thus, he would rather retain the foreign term *tilīfūn* than accept the completely artificial *ishtiqāq* form of *ᵓirzīz*. The decisive factor in the configuration of the modern Arabic language, as far as its vocabulary is concerned, is the acceptance the neologisms attain. To Maḥmūd Taymūr this will be determined not by the broad masses of the Arabic-speaking peoples, but by the educated sector of society, which he sees as the true depository of the modern Arabic language.[14]

We do not intend to give here any exhaustive list of arabicized words. In this respect there exists a valuable contribution in the *Bulletin of the Faculty of Arts*, Cairo

11. Muṣṭafā ᶜAlī, *Muḥāḍarāt ᶜan Maᶜrūf al-Ruṣāfī*, pp. 31–32.

12. Ibid., p. 32.

13. *Minutes*, 1:13. The Academy pronounced itself on the question of *ta*ᶜ*rīb* in its second session, January 31, 1934.

14. Maḥmūd Taymūr, *Mushkilāt al-Lughah al-ᶜArabīyah* (Cairo, 1956), pp. 11–14 especially, but also the entire chapter "Qaḍīyat al-Lughah al-ᶜArabīyah."

University, by Fuʾād Ḥasanayn ʿAlī.[15] A few examples will illustrate both of the above-mentioned trends.

Examples of direct incorporation of non-Arabic words without any intention of assimilation: the French word *retouche*, used by the poet and literary critic ʾIbrāhīm al-ʿUrayyiḍ—"Wa hiya [al-qiṭʿah] baʿdu taḥtāju ʾilā ritūsh."[16]

The term "plastic," as used by Muḥammad Mandūr: "Ẓahara fī al-shiʿr al-madhhab al-bārnāsī [Parnassian] al-qāʾim ʿalā ʿunṣur al-b(i)lāstīk, ʾay al-tajsīm."[17] The important thing about this particular term is that it is used with the meaning of dimensionality. Other modern Arabic authors fail to distinguish this meaning of plasticity and confuse it with that of elasticity, thus rendering it arbitrarily as *murūnah*.[18]

ʿAbd al-Raḥmān Shukrī, not being familiar with Christian Arabic terminology, uses the word *ʾabūkālibs*[19] instead of the corresponding Arabic term *al-ruʾyā*, so frequently employed by Lebanese writers.

ʾAḥmad Zakī ʾAbū Shādī uses the adapted Arabic transliteration of "academic" instead of the then (1933) new term of *majmaʿī*, which lacked the ironic connotation the writer wanted to give while speaking of *mabāḥith ʾakādīmīyah*.[20]

Finally, here are a few examples of completely arabicized loanwords. Behind the perfectly Arabic verbal or nominal forms, the original root is sometimes not even quite transparent: *taʾamraka* (to become American),[21] *maskharah*

15. Fuʾād Ḥasanayn ʿAlī, "Al-Dakhīl fī al-Lughah al-ʿArabīyah," in *Majallat Kullīyat al-ʾĀdāb*, vol. 10, pt. 2 (December 1948), pp. 75–112; vol. 11, pt. 1 (May 1949), pp. 25–26; vol. 11 pt. 2 (December 1949), pp. 1–36; vol. 12, pt. 1 (May 1950), pp. 37–74.

16. ʾIbrāhīm al-ʿUrayyiḍ, and others, *Fī al-ʾAdab al-ʿArabī al-Ḥadīth* (Cairo, 1954), p. 75.

17. Muḥammad Mandūr, *Al-Shiʿr al-Miṣrī baʿda Shawqī* (Cairo, 1955), p. 7.

18. See, for example, the discussion of this term by Ḥasan Ḥusayn Fahmī in his book *Al-Marjiʿ*, p. 33.

19. *Apollo*, 1, no. 10 (June 1933): 1200.

20. *Apollo*, 2, no. 4 (December 1933): 266.

21. Louis Sheikho, *Al-ʾĀdāb al-ʿArabīyah fī al-Rubʿ al-ʾAwwal min al-Qarn al-ʿIshrīn* (Beirut, 1926), p. 138.

(Plural, *maskharāt* or *masākhir*) (masquerade),[22] *munāwarah* (maneuver),[23] and the different derivations from the word *talfazah* (television), such as *talfaza* (to televise), *al-tilfāz* (the television set), constructed according to the mold *mifʿāl*—*ʾidhāʿah talfazīyah* or *mutalfazah* (televised transmission).[24]

22. Wehr, *Dictionary of Modern Arabic.*

23. Ibid.

24. Muṣṭafā al-Shihābī: "Khawāṭir fī al-Qawmīyah al-ʿArabīyah wa al-Lughah al-Fuṣḥā," in *Majallat Majmaʿ al-Lughah al-ʿArabīyah bi Dimashq*, 36, pt. 3 (July 1961):356. Another term for television is that derived from the Arabic root *raʾā* (to see), whence the term *ʾidhāʿah marʾīyah.*

Semantic Developments

4

SEMANTIC changes and developments are an old process in the Arabic language. Since pre-Islamic times until the present moment, the change in meanings of words has been so great that it now requires a special philological background to be able to read and properly understand poets like Imruʾ al-Qays, al-Nābighah, or al-Shanfarā. Not that the vocabulary used by those poets would be utterly strange to a modern reader. On the contrary, most of it seems familiar up to a point where it becomes tempting to forget the barrier of time and to surrender to the illusory idea of being able to identify present-day meanings and concepts with the ancient ones. Soon enough, however, there comes the inevitable disenchantment and the realization that, even though words remain and retain their structure, their meanings are less stable: these waver, change, evolve, or become forgotten and lost. Of course, on behalf of the traditional philological point of view, one could reply that Arabic is a single whole, where the distinctions between old and new matter little, and are a measure of the respective degree of knowledge or ignorance of the language. It is dangerous to sustain such a thesis, however, because ignorance would then become a tragically overwhelming social phenomenon, and would constitute the rule, with knowledge as the exception.

Responsible modernists among the *Nahḍah* intellectuals oppose such a drastic black-and-white projection of the basic problems. To them the evolution of the language is not an arbitrary and hostile movement against traditional values, but a companion phenomenon of the general evolution of society and of the change of environment. Words do not change simply in order to degenerate, as was the assumption of the traditionalists. There are positive aspects to the change too. The fundamental positive attitude towards all change is contained in the concept of evolution (*al-taṭawwur*), which has become one of the most used modern concepts, one behind which the modernists like to shield their sometimes drastic innovatory attitudes. In regard to the language, the argument of evolution in the positive sense is quite often applied even to the emergence of colloquial dialects, to their pressure upon the literary language, and to the subsequent threat of a breach with it. In our present inquiry into the newer semantic developments in the Arabic language we shall not take into account such extreme differences as those existing between the classical meanings and their colloquial offsprings. We shall rather limit ourselves to developments within the modern literary language.

Much of what might be considered as semantic development was already discussed in chapter 1 in the section on *ishtiqāq*. Thus, for example, the basic root *ṭabaᶜa* had first to assume the new meaning of "to print," in order to allow further derivations. Therefore, at the root of most new derivations there lies a modern semantic development. Arabicized expressions, too, like those examined in chapter 6, on foreign modes of expression, very often contain new semantic developments. In most cases new meanings do not introduce any radical changes. They tend rather to be extensions of the basic ideas of the words. In these extensions or broadenings of the meanings, however, there is to be observed a particular tendency towards abstraction and conceptualization. A characteristic and highly instructive example is the development of the very term for abstraction (*tajrīd*). The basic idea of the root *j r d*, as it appears in pre-Islamic poetry, suggests the state of being bare, stripped of something, hairless. Form II of that root (*jarrada*) comes to mean to peep, to strip, to lay bare. Then it undergoes a tentative, initial semantic generalization, meaning to divest a thing of everything accessory, to render it bare. From here, the next step was towards the meaning of physical abstraction and, finally, towards the general concept of abstraction itself.

More recently, Arab linguists began taking notice of this general semantic tendency towards abstraction and conceptualization. ᵓAnīs Furayḥah calls this phenomenon *al-taṣᶜīd*, a form of semantic raising to higher levels:

> With this term we want to designate the capacity of the language for abstraction; that means, the abstraction of the concrete image and its transposition to a conceptual level, or otherwise, the elevation of the concrete word through conceptualization. This is a characteristic which applies to every live, developed language, and Arabic is not less equipped in this respect than other languages.
>
> Who would nowadays associate the word reason (*ᶜaql*) with a rope made of hair which was used to tie a camel's leg? Who would suspect a relationship between glory (*majd*) and the full belly of a beast; or that of soul with the activity of breathing, and of spirit with wind and air? All meanings have their first concrete, tangible stage, but with the progress of life and intellect—and considering the limited number of lexical units—man finds himself obliged to use the old lexicon for new meanings by way of semantic extension.[1]

Another contemporary Arab linguist, ᵓIbrāhīm ᵓAnīs, discusses at some length the evolution of languages from concrete meanings towards abstractions, deriving his gen-

1. ᵓAnīs Furayḥah, *Naḥwa ᶜArabīyatin Muyassarah* (Beirut, 1955), p. 14. Strangely enough, Monteil (*L'arabe moderne*, p. 168) equates Furayḥah's *taṣᶜīd* with *taḍmīn*. In a linguistic sense, as a term, *taḍmīn* is something quite different, not the *contenu implicite* in the broadest sense as understood by Monteil.

eral observations largely from Leonard Bloomfield.[2] To him the trend of semantic abstraction accompanies the evolution of the human mind along the course of its growth and maturation. Although the process of abstraction of the language could be equally considered as a form of its metaphorization, this metaphorization should be distinguished from the strictly literary use of metaphors.

A metaphor as rhetorical figure, of course, produces a semantic extension. In essence, however, the two methods are pursuing different aims. A metaphoric semantic extension creates new images with old verbal means, whereas a semantic abstraction reduces a meaning to its essential concept. Thus, on one hand we get imagery with a still quite restricted expressive range for the lexical components of the metaphor, whereas on the other hand we get conceptualization which is not limited in its expressive semantic scope. The abstract, conceptualized meaning neither necessarily excludes the primary meaning nor the secondary, metaphorical one. It contains all the semantic possibilities of a word in its many aspects.[3]

One need not go beyond classical Arabic to find the process of semantic extension and abstraction in full operation. A verb like *fataḥa*, for example, aside from meaning "to open," came to mean: "to conquer," "to begin," "to judge" (between—*bayna*), "to inform," "to help," and so on. With the exception of the principal meaning, which was originally concrete, all the others constitute the wide scope of semantic extension—some becoming abstract, still others retaining concrete connotations and depending either entirely or partially on a metaphoric context.

Thus the contextual metaphoric use of *fataḥa* appears with an abstract meaning in the koranic verse: Wa law ᵓanna ᵓahla al-qurā ᵓāmanū wa ittaqaw la fataḥnā ᶜalayhim barakātin min al-samāᵓi wa al-ᵓarḍi ("And if the people of those towns had believed and feared [Us], We would have

2. Leonard Bloomfield, *Language* (New York, 1938), pp. 425–43 (chapter on semantic change).

3. ᵓIbrāhīm ᵓAnīs, *Dalālat al-ᵓAlfāẓ* (Cairo, 1963), pp. 161–67. In his differentiation between the metaphoric stage of semantic extension and the conceptualized one, he goes beyond Bloomfield.

surely *bestowed* upon them blessings from heaven and earth").[4]

In another verse the metaphoric use of *fataḥa* is still in its concrete, initial stage, and the "weight" of the abstraction rests on the word *ʾabwāb: fataḥnā ʿalayhim ʾabwāba kulli shayʾin* ("We opened unto them the gates of everything").[5]

A contextual, metaphoric semantic extension of a concrete verb or of its nominal derivatives occurs also in expressions like *rabaṭa jaʾshahu* (to be heartened), *rābiṭ al-jaʾsh* (strong-hearted), *rabṭ al-jaʾsh* (strong-heartedness).

In other verbs, the complete semantic extension and conceptualization have already been accomplished. Such verbs do not need a metaphoric context in order to pass from concrete to abstract. ʾIsmāʿīl Maẓhar calls our attention to the classical abstract semantic extensions of the verb *ʾakhadha* (to take) in expressions like: *lā taʾkhudhuhu sinatun wa lā nawmun* (neither drowsiness nor sleep shall overcome Him); *sinatun taʾkhudhuhā mithlu al-sukri* (sleepiness overcomes her like intoxication); *ʾakhadha al-thawbu al-muzakhrafu al-qulūba maʾkhadhahu* (the ornamented garment captivated the hearts duly).[6]

Characteristic of the koranic tendency to conceptualize basically concrete verbs is the use of *dhāqa* (to taste) in the following complex metaphor: *Wa ʾadhāqahā al-Lāhu libāsa al-jūʿi wa al-khawfi* (So God made her taste the garment of hunger and fear).[7]

Al-Jāḥiẓ uses *taʿaṣṣara* (to be squeezed, expressed) in a clearly abstract sense, with the old metaphoric connotation hardly perceptible at all: *Fa taʿaṣṣara qalīlan thumma bāḥa bi sirrihi* (He constrained himself a little, then came out with his secret);[8] or the verb *khaṭaba* (to ask in marriage), in a context still partially dependent on the meta-

4. *Koran,* Sura VII, 94.
5. Ibid., Sura VI, 44.
6. ʾIsmāʿīl Maẓhar, "Al-Lughah al-ʿArabīyah wa Ḥājatuhā ʾilā Muʿjamin Lughawīyin Taʾrīkhīyin," in: *Al-Majallah,* year 4, no. 4 (April 1960), pp. 21–22.
7. Koran, Sura XVI, 113.
8. Al-Jāḥiẓ, *Al-Bukhalāʾ* (Cairo, 1958), p. 63.

phor: . . . *wa yakhṭubu al-siyādata* (and courts authority).[9]

The concrete meaning of the verb *shaḥana* (to fill, to load, as a ship) has been extended in classical Arabic already, permitting its full abstract use.[10]

It would need a special lexical-historical and stylistic study of the classical language to verify the extent to which the process of abstraction and conceptualization has affected it in its various developmental stages, in its prose or in its poetry. In the earliest formative stages of the language—about which we can have only intimations but no precise knowledge—this process must have been the strongest. Arabic, like other culture-bearing languages, being highly conceptualized, shows nonetheless, almost invariably, root etymologies which point to the tangible and concrete. For our immediate purpose, however, it is more important to observe such semantic shifts towards abstraction as were taking place after the archaic period, in the literary stage of the language. In this stage, then, lexical history is at first history of style. Changes become stylistic phenomena, turning then, progressively, into lexical-historical ones.

Abstract semantic extension in Arabic, however, has had, and still has, its counterprocess as well, the opposite tendency, whereby abstracts become concrete objects, or where abstract verbal references become concrete ones.

Thus, the verb *shaghala* (to occupy, to busy, as to busy anyone in) may be used concretely: *naḥnu nashghalu ʿanka al-martaʿa* (we occupy the place of pasturage so as to keep it from you),[11] or in this even clearer example by al-Jāḥiẓ: *ḥattā yaṣīra kirāʾu al-wāḥidi ka kirāʾi al-ʾalfi, wa taṣīra al-ʾiqāmatu ka al-ẓaʿni wa al-tafrīghu ka al-shughli* (and vacating becomes like occupying [house, apartment]).[12]

This concrete use of *shaghala*, meaning "to occupy, as a place," becomes more frequent in modern Arabic prose. The novelist Najīb Maḥfūẓ says, for example: *wa fī mā*

9. Al-Jāḥiẓ, *Rasāʾil al-Jāḥiẓ*, 1:140.

10. See below, p. 110.

11. Edward William Lane, *Arabic-English Lexicon* (New York, 1955).

12. Al-Jāḥiẓ, *Al-Bukhalāʾ*, p. 89.

warāʾahumā tantathiru al-qubūru fa tashghalu masāḥatan min al-ʾarḍi lā yuḥīṭu bihā al-baṣaru (and [the graves] occupy an area of land).[13]

The concretization becomes even more obvious in cases where *maṣdar*-type abstractions turn into concrete substantives. Hans Wehr points out as modern examples: *ʾījāzāt* (*Mieten*); *ʾiʿānāt* (*Beihilfen, finanzielle Beiträge*); *ʾīrādāt* (*Einkünfte*).[14]

The process of semantic extension, one may thus say, is made possible by a general openness of meaning, and is not to be seen as a simple shift from concrete to abstract (mostly) or from abstract to concrete (less frequently), but rather as an increasingly conceptualized concentration of meaning in a word, without any qualifications beyond the concept. The way towards this essential meaning, as we already observed, leads through the metaphor.

Before turning to specifically modern illustrations of semantic extension in the above sense, we should remind the reader that many of the neologisms considered in the chapter on *ishtiqāq*—particularly of the kind where an approximation of older vocabulary to new meanings takes place (*al-waḍʿ bi al-majāz*)—constitute a very precise form of semantic extension as well.[15] The nominal derivatives which are thus obtained, however, mostly refer to clearly defined, concrete individual meanings and do not constitute unlimited semantic extensions in the sense with which the present chapter is concerned.

To our category of modern semantic extensions through abstraction belong the following words, selected from various, although mostly literary, materials.

The verbs *taḥaddara* and *inḥadara*, whose meaning is "to descend, slowly or gradually," have broadened that meaning, which originally was limited to the physical act of descending or coming down the slope, so that it now includes the temporal idea of coming down, being handed

13. Najīb Maḥfūẓ, *Zuqāq al-Midaqq*, p. 224.

14. Hans Wehr, "Entwicklung und traditionelle Pflege der arabischen Schriftsprache in der Gegenwart," in *Zeitschrift der Deutschen Morgenländischen Gesellschaft*, 97 (1943): 42.

15. See above: pp. 30–34, especially.

down by time: *wa qad taḥaddarat ʾilā ʿahdin qarībin minnā* (and it had come down to an epoch close to ours);[16] or: *wa ʾidhā inḥadarnā ʾilā al-qarnayni al-ʾakhīrayni* (and when we descended to the last two centuries);[17] or another example: *wa hiya (al-kalimatu) rubbamā inḥadarat ʾilaynā min saḥīqi al-ʿuṣūri* (a word which probably came down to us from remote ages).[18]

But the new, extended use of *inḥadara* is not always temporal. It can be as broadly figurative as that of its counterparts in some European languages: *fa tanḥadiru (lughatu al-taqlīdi) bi shāʿirīyatihi ʾilā al-mubālaghāti al-khāwiyati* (the language of imitation *degrades* his poetic quality to hollow exaggerations).[19]

The discussion which developed on the pages of the review *Apollo* (1933) around ʾAḥmad Zakī ʾAbū Shādī's abstract use of the verb *dhāqa* (to taste) in his verse—

> *Yadrī bihi al-ʿushshāqu ʾin lam yadrihi*
> *man lam yadhuq marʾāki ʾaw maʿnāki*
> (one who has not savored the sight of you or
> the meaning of you)—

shows us, on the one hand, that such usages were considered as innovations stemming from foreign sources and, on the other hand, that there was little awareness of older developments in this direction, and that only direct parallels with a classical example—preferably a koranic one (Sura XVI, 113)—could sufficiently justify such a usage.[20]

Common current extended usages are: *tabādala* (to exchange mutually, as greetings or sentiments); *ʾaʿāra* (to lend, as attention, interest); *ʾazhara* or *izdahara* (to flourish, as a civilization or friendship); *tabalwara* (to crystallize, as hopes or ideas);[21] and so on.

The verb *ʿakasa*, which originally conveyed only the action of returning or throwing back something concrete,

16. Al-Maqdisī, *Al-Ittijāhāt al-ʾAdabīyah*, p. 302.
17. Ibid., p. 377.
18. Ḥusayn Muruwwah, *Qaḍāyā ʾAdabīyah* (Cairo, 1956), p. 45.
19. Mandūr, *Al-Shiʿr baʿda Shawqī*, p. 26.
20. *Apollo* 2, no. 4 (December 1943):279, 283; ibid. 2, no. 5:362.
21. See below, pp. 101, 102, 110.

came to mean: "to return or reflect, as the light," and finally, "to reflect," in an abstract as well as general sense.[22]

The classical Arabic meaning of *nazafa* applies to the draining of blood or of water from a well; it then comes to be used for the drying up of tears. In modern Arabic, semantic extension allows an abstract use of this root, without any clear indication of a metaphor: *wa furūḍu al-durūsi tastanzifu al-waqta* (and the duties of studies consume time).[23]

Similarly, the old meaning of *naḍaba* (to sink into the ground, as water; to have little milk, as a she-camel) becomes generalized: *kāna yabkī khayālan naḍaba* (he wept over an imagination that dried up).[24] Or as in the extension of the usage of the verb *naḍaḥa* (originally: to exude water, to sweat): *thumma iltafatat ṣawba al-nāfidhati fa raʾat khaṣāṣahā yanḍaḥu bi ḍawʾi al-ḍuḥā* (then she turned towards the window and saw its opening flow over with the light of forenoon).[25] Or as in the verb *washā* (to embroider, as a garment; to adorn something), which has passed through a first metaphoric extension, *washā al-kalāma bi al-zūri* (to adorn one's words with falsehood), and then simply, *washā al-kalāma*. A further extension (with the preposition *bi*) produces the meaning "to misrepresent," "to accuse falsely," and then "to betray." In contemporary usage this last meaning becomes abstracted from concrete reference, as in the expression: *fa qāla al-ghulāmu bi ṣawtin yashī bi iḥtijājihi ʿalā sūʾi muqābalatihā lahu* (the boy spoke with a voice betraying his protest against the bad reception she gave him).[26]

Verbs that have undergone such extensions of usage also

22. Al-Maqdisī, *Al-Ittijāhāt al-ʾAdabīyah*, p. 302. The further derivations of this broad meaning of "to reflect" result in such modern terms as *al-ḥarakah al-inʿikāsīyah* (reflexive movement), and so forth.

23. Sulaymān al-Bustānī, *ʾIlyādhat Hūmīrūs*, p. 68.

24. Najīb Maḥfūẓ, *Qaṣr al-Shawq*, p. 67.

25. Najīb Maḥfūẓ, *Bayna al-Qaṣrayni* (Cairo, 1956), p. 161.

26. Ibid., p. 145. There may also be a remote etymological or onomatopoeically phonetic relationship between the root *washā* and *washwasha* or *waswasa*.

produce their respective, semantically extended nominal infinitive forms, participles, and *nisbah*-adjectives: *fa Faraḥu al-qawīyu al-khayāli al-mughadhdhā bi al-qirāʾati al-dasimati* (and Faraḥ, of strong imagination, nourished by abundant reading).[27] The participial expression "nourished by reading," implying an abstract verbal extension, is new in Arabic.

Thus also in this *nisbah*-adjective built upon a *maṣdar*, which presupposes extended *maṣdar* and verbal meanings of *ightaṣaba: fa tabassama tabassuman ightiṣābīyan* (and he smiled with a forced smile).[28]

The adjective *ṣāmid*, with its meaning of "solid," but also "enduring," "eternal," and then "defiant," constitutes more than a semantic extension. It is also a new *ishtiqāq* form. Thus in the verses by Nāzik al-Malāʾikah:

> *Jubtuhā kullahā wa ʿadūwī al-khafīyu al-ʿanīd*
> *Ṣāmidun ka jibāli al-jalīd*
> *Ṣāmidun ka ṣumūdi al-nujūm*
> (I traversed it all, with my secret, relentless enemy
> Solid and defiant like glaciers
> Enduring and defiant like the stars.)[29]

Both the participial adjective *ṣāmid* and the *maṣdar* *ṣumūd* imply a corresponding new semantic extension of the verb *ṣamada*, which, in fact, exists in contemporary usage with the meaning of "to stand up, as against someone," "to defy," "to brave," "to withstand."[30]

Other nonverbal abstract extensions need not entail or depend upon verbal ones. Thus, in the expression *bayna mukhtalifi al-quṣūri* (among various palaces),[31] *quṣūr* has

27. Mārūn ʿAbbūd, *Judud wa Qudamāʾ* (Beirut, 1954), p. 59. Notice also the abstract extension of the adjective *dasim*.

28. Jurjī Zaydān, *ʾAsīr al-Mutamahdī*, 4th ed. (Cairo, 1924), p. 24.

29. The verses come from al-Malāʾikah's poem "*Al-ʾUfʿuwān*," included in the collection *Shaẓāyā wa Ramād;* see their discussion in connection with the use of *ṣāmid* in ʾIbrāhīm al-Sāmarrāʾī's *Lughat al-Shiʿr*, p. 186.

30. Wehr, *Dictionary of Modern Arabic.*

31. Muḥammad ʿAbd al-Lāh ʿInān, *Dawlat al-ʾIslām fī al-ʾAndalus —Al-ʿAṣr al-ʾAwwal* (Cairo, 1960), pt. 1, p. 278. Notice, however, the analogy with the classical extension of *bayt*, as it acquires the meaning of "family," in *The Nakāʾid of Jarīr and al-Farazdak* (Leiden, 1905), 1:87.

acquired the meaning of "royal houses or families," "monarchies."

In the expression *ẓilālu al-maᶜānī* (the shades, or tones, of meanings),[32] the abstract extension of the meaning of *ẓill* went beyond the stage of its older metaphorically based meaning of "refuge."

In modern Arabic the adjective *ḥamīm* came to signify "intimate." Among its old meanings with concrete references the notion closest to "intimate" is that of "a close relation or friend for whom one cares." It was from this meaning that the modern one was derived and generalized abstractly: *ᵓAmmā al-Yūnānu fa lam yaᶜrifhumu al-ᶜArabu hādhihi al-maᶜrifata al-ḥamīmata* (the Arabs did not know them with such *intimate knowledge*).[33]

A far-reaching semantic extension underlies the term for the abstract concept of "positive" (*waḍᶜī*). The root *waḍaᶜa* gave the idea of "to put down," "to locate." Furthermore, the noun *waḍᶜ* (position, situation [of something]) also suggested the meaning of position as manner or attitude. The next step in the logic of derivation gives the *nisbah*-formation of *waḍᶜī* as "positive"—related to position, manner—and makes possible the equation of meaning with the sought-for new concept. Thus we read in Mīkhāᵓīl Nuᶜaymah: *ḥattā yamīla bi baṣarihi ᶜan jihati al-ḥayāti al-salbīyati ᵓilā jihatihā al-waḍᶜīyati; wa Jubrān qad khaṭā khutwatan kabīratan min al-salbīyāti ᵓilā al-waḍᶜīyāti* (until it turned his eyes away from the negative side of life, towards its positive side; thus Jubrān has taken a long step from negative towards positive attitudes).[34] It should be remarked that this meaning of *waḍᶜī*, as an antonym of *salbī*, is in the process of being replaced by the synonym *ᵓījābī*. But *waḍᶜī* still retains the technical meaning of "positivistic" in relation to that particular philosophical school.

The poetess Nāzik al-Malāᵓikah is particularly fond of reducing adjectives, which originally denoted specific

32. Al-Maqdisī, *Al-Ittijāhāt al-ᵓAdabīyah*, p. 407.

33. Mūsā Sulaymān, *Al-ᵓAdab al-Qaṣaṣī ᶜinda al-ᶜArab* (Beirut, 1956), p. 10.

34. Mīkhāᵓīl Nuᶜaymah, *Al-Ghirbāl*, p. 202. Notice also the parallel example of *salbī* (negative).

qualities, to their essential conceptual meaning and then using them out of their conventional contexts, as symbolic correspondences:

> *Mā ʾaḥabba al-masīra wa laysa warāʾī khuṭā māʾitah*
> *Tatamaṭṭā bi ʾaṣdāʾihā al-bāhitah*
> (How I love to walk, without dead steps behind me
> Drawing out their pale echoes).[35]

Here the adjective *bāhit*, regardless of its complex metaphoric context, has an independent, extended meaning and a new, in the Arabic language, dimension of usage.

Similarly in the following verse:

> *Wa inḥanat fawqanā al-shujayrātu ḥuznan*
> *tatabākā bi ʾadmuʿin kharsāʾ*
> (The shrubs bent over us in sadness,
> weeping with mute tears).[36]

The expression *ʾadmuʿ kharsāʾ* (mute tears), being itself figurative, shows that the adjective *kharsāʾ* has acquired a degree of semantic flexibility which frees it from the traditional metaphor. In the words of the critic ʾIbrāhīm al-Sāmarrāʾī, "it enters into the sphere of new metaphors, introduced by the young generation of poets, with Nāzik amongst them. The gate of the metaphor is thus wide open."[37] This new approach to the language, says the same writer, "has impressed the work of those poets with a new stamp."[38]

A new extension of usage has also taken place in the word *ʾābid* (wild). Of limited documentation in pre-Islamic poetry, it suggested the wildness of animals only. With this meaning it occurs, probably for the first time, in the *Muʿallaqah* of Imruʾ al-Qays:

> *Wa qad ʾaghtadī wa al-ṭayru fī wukunātihā*
> *bi munjaridin qaydi al-ʾawābidi haykali.*

It is then used mostly substantivally: *ʾābidah, ʾawābid* (pl.) (a wild beast). Even when Ḍiyāʾ al-Dīn Ibn al-ʾAthīr

35. From Nāzik al-Malāʾikah's *Shaẓāyā wa Ramād*. The verse is quoted and discussed in al-Sāmarrāʾī's *Lughat al-Shiʿr*, p. 187.

36. Nāzik al-Malāʾikah, *ʿĀshiqat al-Layl*, 2d. ed. (Beirut, 1960), p. 15.

37. ʾIbrāhīm al-Sāmarrāʾī, *Lughat al-Shiʿr*, p. 163.

38. Ibid., p. 188.

(died A.H. 637) uses it in an abstract metaphoric context, as in *qallamā yakhtilu al-muʾallifu bi sharaki fikrihi ʾawābida ʾalfāẓihi* (rarely does the author snare his thought on the wild beasts of its words),[39] no permanent extension of usage takes place. Basically the *ʾawābid* of Ibn al-ʾAthīr still needs the prop of the implied concrete reference to Imruʾ al-Qays. Modern Arabic has gone further, inasmuch as it has achieved the isolation of *ʾābid* from any archaic metaphoric allusion. Now this adjective has come to mean "wild" in the entire semantic range, abstract as well as concrete. Thus the modern Tunisian poet, ʾAbū al-Qāsim al-Shābbī, feels free to say:

> *Ṭāqāti wardin ʾābidin tuzrī bi ʾawrādi al-quṣūr*
> (Bouquets of wild roses that scorn the roses of palaces).[40]

While only thirty years ago semantic transpositions and abstractions in poetic language were still viewed with suspicion, present-day poets find the way open to such usages. Moreover, whereas the poetic language of the past generation was still more controlled and conservative than the language of prose in this respect, now poetry is forcing prose into accepting its more daring lexicon.

39. Ḍiyāʾ al-Dīn Ibn al-ʾAthīr, *Al-Jāmiʿ al-Kabīr fī Ṣināʿat al-Manẓūm min al-Kalām wa al-Manthūr* (Baghdad, 1956), 263.
40. ʾAbū al-Qāsim al-Shābbī, *ʾAghānī al-Ḥayāh*, pp. 130–31.

Attempts at a Simplification of the Grammar

5

THE idea that Arabic grammar, as well as other aspects of the language, needs to be simplified is recent. If we keep in mind, however, that in its early stages the modernization of the language was above all a pragmatic movement, with little theoretical groundwork, we shall find it natural that there should not have been any serious early considerations about grammar. Besides, the belief in classical Arabic philology was until quite recently one of the firmest and most uncompromising of dogmas. In a sense, it was easier to be an outright rebel, to disclaim the very validity of classical Arabic and to champion the cause of the colloquial language, than to try to compromise with classical philology on a theoretical basis. Only after World War I, or rather during the remarkable decade of the twenties, were more voices raised in concern over the rigidity of classical philological canons and the often absurd ways of their presentation. Among these voices the most urgent were those of Jubrān Khalīl Jubrān, Mīkhāʾīl Nuʿaymah, Salāmah Mūsā, Muḥammad Ḥusayn Haykal, and Ṭaha Ḥusayn. We see, for example, how Ṭaha Ḥusayn, himself an "Azharite," passionately protests against being thus labeled. Accused of not having forgotten his grammar lessons, he declares that he harbors "no stronger wish than to forget them."[1] In his autobiographical reminiscences, *Al-ᵓAyyām* (1929), he lays bare the deficiencies of antiquarian methods of language instruction. As we shall see, Ṭaha Ḥusayn's interest in a revision of the old approaches to Arabic grammar does not diminish with the years, even though his position among the modernists may now seem one of restraint and moderation.

As a result of the de facto modernization of the language which was making constant progress, as well as under the influence of the ever livelier debate over the need for a theoretical reappraisal of the old grammatical laws and rules, we find that a decade later, in the thirties, the Egyptian Ministry of Education even created a committee for the study of a possible simplification of grammatical and rhetorical-stylistic rules (*taysīr qawāᶜid al-naḥw wa al-ṣarf wa al-balāghah*).[2] This official concern for the problem further enlivened the discussion, yet it did not produce any decisive change with regard to the old methodology and—which is much more important—it did not create the means for a true simplification of the grammar. The official grammar textbook for Egypt's public schools had been for some time already the *Kitāb Qawāᶜid al-Lughah al-ᶜArabīyah*, arranged by a number of prominent Egyptian philologists and educators. Yet neither the contents nor the organization of this material revealed new approaches.

Therefore, when the Syrian Sāṭiᶜ al-Ḥuṣrī, challenged by the goals projected by the Egyptian Committee mentioned above, enters into the discussion over the simplification of the Arabic grammar,[3] he proposes that the first task in a reform of the grammar be a thorough revision of the old methodologies, a redefinition of grammatical terms and categories, a reclassification and regrouping of the not always logically organized traditional system of basic

1. Ṭaha Ḥusayn, *Ḥadīth al-ᵓArbaᶜāᵓ*, 3:111. The essay in question is one of Ṭaha Ḥusayn's dialogues with M. Ḥ. Haykal on the pages of *Al-Siyāsah al-ᵓUsbūᶜīyah*.

2. Presumably in 1938. See al-Ḥuṣrī, *ᵓĀrāᵓ wa ᵓAḥādīth*, p. 84.

3. Ibid., pp. 83–113.

grammatical rules. New scientific methods must be observed in such a reform, based upon objective reason and logic, and the pedagogical purpose must be kept in view. "This is," says al-Ḥuṣrī, "what I should like to appeal for to scholars and writers . . . and I believe that reform in this direction ought to be the first step taken towards simplification."[4]

To begin with, Sāṭiᶜ al-Ḥuṣrī draws the distinction between the specific characteristics of a language and its philological rules. The rules are not inflexible, for they are the product of a particular way of thinking in a particular time and should therefore not be accepted without critical revision. His criticism is aimed directly at the above-mentioned official school version of Arabic grammar (*Qawāᶜid al-Lughah al-ᶜArabīyah*), which repeats most of the logical misconceptions of the old grammarians.

He would like to apply the method and the logic of Western philology to Arabic grammar. For example, he would abolish the traditional division of words into nouns, verbs, and particles and, instead, adopt the classical Western system. He would separate from the traditional Arabic concept of the noun (*ism*) the adjective, the pronoun, the infinitive (*maṣdar*) and the participles, establishing the adjective and the pronoun independently as well as broadening the Arabic concept of the verb by the incorporation of the infinitive and the participles. Furthermore, he would add the future tense to the three traditional categories of past tense, present tense, and imperative, and define clearly the composite verb (*fiᶜl murakkab*) or the auxiliary function of *kāna* and related verbs. By means of these reforms, Sāṭiᶜ al-Ḥuṣrī does not expect to simplify the Arabic language as such. He only hopes to make its texture more transparent and its internal logic more evident.

Almost two decades later (1955), Sāṭiᶜ al-Ḥuṣrī returned to the problem of simplification of the language in the Introduction he wrote to a book by ʾAnīs Furayḥah.[5]

4. Ibid., pp. 110–11.

5. ʾAnīs Furayḥah, *Al-Lahajāt wa ʾUslūb Dirāsatihā* (Cairo, 1955).

Yet, this time it is no longer the discipline of grammar alone which needs simplification. The language itself, he feels, has to be simplified. This should be brought about through an approximation of the classical language to the colloquial dialects. The basic question al-Ḥuṣrī asks is:

> Could we not ingraft the colloquial languages with the classical language in a way which would save us from the pedantry of the philologists and the gibberish of the common people at the same time, and which would lead us to an intermediate and moderate literary language? Would it not be better for us to resort to this method, even if it were on a temporary basis, as a stage in our progress towards perfect classical?[6]

He knows that such a simplification of the language is not an easy enterprise. Moreover, it would require a previous study of many factors, such as a sufficiently precise establishment of the limits between the literary language and the different colloquial dialects, and a thorough study not only of the literary grammatical rules, but also of the intricacies of the vernacular dialects. However remote this goal of a theoretical simplification of the language may be, al-Ḥuṣrī already sees some positive accomplishments in the field of linguistic practice, where there is developing a unified conversational language among the educated classes which is neither purely literary nor utterly vernacular. This new development might be a trend worth observing and studying.[7]

The new and rather spontaneous trend in the spoken language towards a semiclassical *koine* of the educated classes, however, should not be confused with the artificial proposition to create a sort of "basic Arabic," which would be an idiom reduced in vocabulary and highly simplified in grammar, understandable to every Arab and which would

6. Al-Ḥuṣrī, *ʾĀrāʾ wa ʾAḥādīth*, p. 44.

7. Ibid., p. 48. The Lebanese linguist ʾAnīs Furayḥah does precisely that in his book *Naḥwa ʿArabīyatin Muyassarah*, pp. 183–96. He proposes to fix grammatically and phonetically that intermediate language which today is frequently used by most educated Arabs. His concern with phonetic precision makes him favor an adaptation of the Latin script.

serve for the elementary needs of communication. The prototype of this extremely simplified language would be the idea of the so-called "basic English." From the very beginning the creation of "basic Arabic" proved to be an abortive attempt. It was almost universally repudiated. Maḥmūd Taymūr rejects it not only as impracticable, but as a threat to further literary progress; this neoprimitivism would not constitute progress, only retrogression.[8]

On the whole, purely theoretical approaches to the problem of reforming Arabic grammar very seldom contribute any positive and useful solutions or even suggestions. As a rule, after an initial introductory paragraph about the need for reform and about the stagnation and sterility of the traditional methods applied to Arabic grammar, the would-be reformer relapses into the same conservative position which he presumably was going to demolish once and for all. An example of this practice is furnished by the Iraqi Muṣṭafā Jawād, whose second article in the series entitled "Wasāʾil al-Nuhūḍ bi al-Lughah al-ʿArabīyah wa Taysīr Qawāʿidihā wa Kitābatihā" appeared in the review *Al-ʾUstādh*.[9] The article starts in the usual grandiloquent style of promising total reform. Alas, when the author arrives at the point where he must define his position, we see that his reform program is rather disenchantingly familiar.

> In my opinion the general method which leads towards the reform of grammar consists in the reduction of the basic rules and the selection of examples, above all from the Noble Koran, then from the Prophetic Tradition of secondary transmission, then from the Arabic prose of the proverbs, the Days [of the Arabs] and the *maqāmas*, then from pre-Islamic poetry of authentic origin, unmarred by any corruptions—the clearest criterion of corruption being its incongruity with Arabic prose of whatever kind—finally from post-*Jāhilī* poetic selections.[10]

Considerably more interesting are those approaches to the reform of the grammar which start from more realistic

8. Maḥmūd Taymūr, *Mushkilāt*, p. 16.
9. *Al-ʾUstādh* 8 (1960): 136–54.
10. Ibid., p. 137.

premises. One of these premises is the existence of vernacular languages which, until very recently, monopolized spoken discourse. Another premise is the disappearance for most practical purposes of the *ʾiʿrāb* or desinential flection, to the extent that it is not even mentally taken into account in ordinary reading. In a special way, the problem of the *ʾiʿrāb* must bear strongly upon every consideration of grammatical reform, because the main part of Arabic grammar concerns itself with desinential flections.

We know that already in the first century of Islam transgressions against the *ʾiʿrāb* were common even among true Arabs. During the subsequent centuries of conquest and urbanization, the *ʾiʿrāb* remains as the distinctive characteristic of the Bedouin speech only, while the heterogeneous population of the cities tends to abandon it or rather is never able to learn it. Finally, on the outer threshold of Arabic cultural decline, Ibn Khaldūn (A.D. 1332–1406) writes that "contemporary Arabic is an independent language, different from the languages of the Muḍar and Ḥimyar."[11] This difference was brought about, according to Ibn Khaldūn, by the complete neglect of the *ʾiʿrāb*.

> We find that with regard to clear indication of what one wants to express and full expression of meaning, Arabic (as it is spoken today) follows the ways of the Muḍar language. The only loss is that of the vowels indicating the distinction between subject and object. Instead, one uses position within the sentence and syntactic combinations [*qarāʾin*] to indicate certain special meanings one wants to express. . . .[12]

Then he reiterates his point and becomes more explicit:

> The only part of the codified language that no longer exists is the *ʾiʿrāb*, the vowel endings that were used in the language of the Muḍar in a uniform and definite manner and which form part of the laws of [the Arabic] language.[13]

11. Ibn Khaldūn, *Al-Muqaddimah*, ed. M. Quatremère (1858), 3:299; tr. Franz Rosenthal (1958), 3:344. In the following quotations we shall mostly adopt the translation of Professor Rosenthal.

12. Ibid., 3:299 (Arabic text); 3:344 (Rosenthal).

13. Ibid., 3:301 (Arabic text); 3:346 (Rosenthal).

After explaining in general terms the birth of the philological sciences among the Arabs, how the codification of the language was necessary in order to preserve its original purity, and how philology became a rigorous discipline, indispensable for the comprehension of the Koran and the *Sunnah* of the Prophet, Ibn Khaldūn proceeds with the problem of the *ʾiʿrāb:*

> Perhaps, if we were to concern ourselves with the present-day Arabic language and probe into its laws, we would replace the desinential vowels, whose meaning has become corrupted, by other things and by properties, implicitly present in the language, which would have their peculiar laws and perhaps would follow in the word-endings a method different from that which originally existed in the language of the Muḍar. Languages and [linguistic] habits are not matters of chance.[14]

According to Ibn Khaldūn, there are analogies between the Ḥimyarite language and the language of the Muḍar, and between that of the Muḍar and contemporary Arabic. The difference is that, whereas the religious law had caused scholars in the past to evolve and derive the philological rules of the language of the Muḍar, "there is nothing nowadays to move us to do the same [for present-day Arabic]."[15]

Yet, what was true in the time of Ibn Khaldūn is no longer true for many modernists of the present *Nahḍah.* The Egyptian writer and educator ʾAḥmad ʾAmīn picks up the thread of Ibn Khaldūn's considerations on the *ʾiʿrāb* and the emergence of a distinctive contemporary language and proposes to elaborate that language and to give it its own rules. For ʾAḥmad ʾAmīn the main difference between the colloquial dialects and the classical language, as well as the principal difficulty in the spread of the literary language, is the *ʾiʿrāb:*

> We have failed to teach it [the *ʾiʿrāb*] even to the educated minority; and there you have our university

14. Ibid., 3:301–2 (Arabic text); 3:347 (Rosenthal). I found myself obliged to change several things in Rosenthal's version, however.
15. Ibid., 3:302 (Arabic text); 3:347–48 (Rosenthal).

> graduates who spend at least nine years in primary and secondary schools studying grammar, then a number of years at the university, and, in spite of it, very rarely are they able to write a page free of grammatical errors. This being the case with broadly educated people who have read much by themselves and written much, how then can we aspire to attain any convincing results by spreading the instruction of the Arabic language in lower social media . . . ?[16]

In order to remedy this state, ᵓAḥmad ᵓAmīn proposes to develop a language which would not only assimilate the positive elements of the vernacular idiom and free itself of the burden of pedantic vocabulary, but which above everything else would abolish the desinential flections, and thus simplify the very foundations of the language. This new language would be truly intermediary between the *al-fuṣḥā* and the *al-ᶜāmmīyah*, "and it is upon it," proceeds ᵓAḥmad ᵓAmīn, "that we should rely for the spread of education among common people. Thus we shall be able to bring together colloquial and literary and also facilitate the study of the Arabic language in its high form, in which specialists will write for the specialists, and in which the ancient heritage will be studied and then discriminately translated into the new language for the benefit of the general public. This new language will be a suitable vehicle for literature as creative art in all the genres and classes."[17]

The breaking away from the *ᵓiᶜrāb*, however, would require the change of certain fundamental syntactical rules. Thus, for example, the desinential flection determines the distinction between subject and object in such a sentence as: *ᵓaqraḍa Muḥammadun ᶜAlīyan* (M. lent money to A.). Even if we change the order of the words (*ᵓaqraḍa ᶜAlīyan Muḥammadun*), this distinction remains. Without the *ᵓiᶜrāb*, however, it would be impossible to establish with complete certainty the true subject and object.[18] There-

16. ᵓAḥmad ᵓAmīn: "Mustaqbal al-ᵓAdab al-ᶜArabī," in *Al-Thaqāah*, year 6, no. 280 (1944), pp. 6–7.

17. Ibid., p. 6.

18. For the very same reason ᵓAḥmad ᵓAmīn's contemporary, ᶜAbbās Maḥmūd al-ᶜAqqād, maintains that it is precisely the *ᵓiᶜrāb* that should be retained in the language, since it facilitates under-

fore, ᵓAḥmad ᵓAmīn proposes to change the syntactic rule which demands that in a verbal sentence the verb should go before the noun. The subject should be allowed to stand first, followed by the verbal predicate and then by the direct object without *ᵓiᶜrāb*. Both subject and object would thus be without any distinction of inflection except for their position (as in the sentence *Muḥammad ᵓaqraḍ ᶜAlī*). Such a practice, however, if established as the main rule concerning the order of words in a verbal predicate sentence, would disrupt the classical structure of the verbal sentence and consequently affect some of the basic notions of Arabic syntax.[19]

Another school of reformers sees as the only viable method of improving and fortifying the language a return to the *ᵓiᶜrāb* and to its close observance in speech as well as writing.[20] They claim that modern methods of education and modern means of information could facilitate a return to the linguistic habit of the *ᵓiᶜrāb*. The main burden in this task would fall upon public education and upon the printed word. The possibilities of public education in this regard are obvious.[21] As for the art of printing, its contribution

standing instead of obstructing it. See his argumentation in the article entitled "Ḥarb al-Lughah" in the review *Al-Kitāb* 11, no. 5 (May 1952):536–40.

19. Some modern philologists, for example ᵓIbrāhīm Muṣṭafā, consider that, contrary to the rigid insistence of the classical grammarians (mainly of the school of Basra) upon the inflexibility of the verbal sentence, the actual linguistic practice of the Arabs shows, on the contrary, that an inversion of the order of words is perfectly licit. See ᵓIbrāhīm Muṣṭafā, *ᵓIḥyāᵓ al-Naḥw* (Cairo, 1937), pp. 55–56.

20. As early a voice as that of Rifāᶜah al-Ṭahṭāwī had already propagated the idea of a new acquisition of the linguistic habit of the classical speech. See Naffūsah Zakariyā Saᶜīd, *Taᵓrīkh al-Daᶜwah ᵓilā al-ᶜĀmmīyah wa ᵓĀthāruhā fī Miṣr* (Alexandria, 1964), p. 77.

21. Muḥammad ᶜArafah, in a book entitled *Mushkilat al-Lughah al-ᶜArabīyah* (1947), suggests that teaching of classical Arabic and its reinstitution as a spoken language should rely on the development of a linguistic habit and not on instruction in grammar. The study of grammar should become the final phase of language instruction, after the students have assimilated the language through direct and continuous exposure to it. See the discussion of his ideas in Naffūsah Zakariyā Saᶜīd, *Al-Daᶜwah*, pp. 197–200.

towards the eventual regaining of the habit of the *ʾiʿrāb* would consist in the introduction of complete vocalization into everything that is published, from scientific treatises to the daily newspaper.

Among the champions of this movement we find such prominent figures as the philologist ʾIbrāhīm Muṣṭafā, and the writers Ṭaha Ḥusayn and Maḥmūd Taymūr. ʾIbrāhīm Muṣṭafā, who was one of the coauthors of the already mentioned textbook, *Qawāʿid al-Lughah al-ʿArabīyah,* is also the author of an interesting philological treatise, *ʾIḥyāʾ al-Naḥw* (Cairo, 1937), where he tries to see classical Arabic grammar in a new critical light. Even though the results of his quest are not revolutionary, his book constitutes one of the few refreshing modern approaches to classical grammar, and particularly to the question of *ʾiʿrāb*.[22] On the whole, however, he looks rather for redefinitions than for actual changes.

Of special interest concerning our immediate topic is ʾIbrāhīm Muṣṭafā's project of an adjustment of the Arabic script in order to make it phonetically more precise. In essence the adjustment would consist in a much broader use of the *al-ʾalif al-mamdūdah* (the lengthened *ʾalif*). Thus, in words like *hadhā* (*hādhā*), *hadhihi* (*hādhihi*), *dhalika* (*dhālika*), *hahunā* (*hāhunā*), where the *ʾalif mamdūdah* is not written out, he gives it back its etymologically long form. Furthermore, he changes the *al-ʾalif al-maqṣūrah* (abbreviated *ʾalif*) of words like *muṣṭafā, maʿnā, jadwā, ḥattā, ʾilā,* into *al-ʾalif al-mamdūdah,* thus making the spelling completely phonetic.[23] This adjustment should be considered as part of the process towards complete vocalization of the Arabic script.

22. He would include under the category of *ʾiʿrāb* the nominative and the genitive only. The accusative, being a circumstantial case, occurs either where the other cases are not in place, or it is an idiomatic phenomenon. Thus the accusative, which receives so much attention by classical grammarians, loses emphasis and becomes much less of a burden for the student of the language.

23. In 1935 the Cairo Academy had already recommended that the phonetic writing of *miʾah* should be followed, but this recommendation was not effective. See *Minutes,* 2:266.

Ṭaha Ḥusayn, in full agreement and close cooperation with ʾIbrāhīm Muṣṭafā, relies in his demand for complete vocalization upon pedagogical arguments. A script without vocalization dissociates the letter from its phonetic value, and thus writing and reading become two disciplines which have to be taught separately. Furthermore, "this also means that we turn writing and reading into goals, and understanding into the means towards those goals."[24] The result of this perversion of values is general ignorance of the language and the difficult task of combating that ignorance.

Maḥmūd Taymūr, who in the course of his own literary career has passed through several stages of conversion to the classical speech, shows even more conviction and faith in the possibility of reeducation of the Arabic-speaking peoples towards the *ʾiʿrāb*. Bent upon facilitating the practical conditions for such a reeducation, he explores in his book *Mushkilāt al-Lughah al-ʿArabīyah* the technical difficulties of printing fully vocalized texts, and finds that this would require a reduction of the different forms of letter-matrices which in the present circumstances exceed the number of three hundred. After reviewing briefly all the different attempts at modifying the Arabic script,[25] he explains and illustrates his own proposed solution, which consists in retaining the initial form of each letter only. This would reduce the overall number of the printer's matrices to about fifty, and thus render easy and economical even completely vocalized editions. An important aspect of this reform would be the essential preservation of the classical script.[26]

We shall not explore any further the many interesting problems connected with Arabic script because to do so would be to overstep the limits of this present chapter. We have mentioned the problems here only because they

24. Ṭaha Ḥusayn, *Min ʾAdabinā al-Muʿāṣir* (Cairo, 1959), p. 47, but see also pp. 45–52.

25. Maḥmūd Taymūr, *Mushkilāt*, pp. 57–62.

26. Ibid., pp. 72–84.

seemed related to broader reforms or counterreforms of the language.[27]

Besides these discussions and broad, general plans of reform, there are minor processes of simplification going on unnoticed in the language. Thus, for example, there is a definite tendency to reduce the sometimes perplexing number of possible plural forms of the noun to a single one or, in isolated cases, to two. Typical examples are: *wādin* (valley), whose confusing profusion of plurals (at least five) in the classical language tends to be reduced in modern usage to two only, *widyān* and *ʾawdiyah; ʿaduww* (enemy), formerly four plurals, now one, *ʾaʿdāʾ*; *jafn* (eyelid), formerly three plurals, now one, *jufūn; jazīrah* (island), formerly two plurals, now one, *juzur.*[28]

Another tendency is to differentiate the gender concordance of *ʾayy* (which, which one). In classical Arabic *ʾayy* is used indiscriminately with nouns of masculine and feminine concordances.[29] In modern Arabic, on the contrary, its use with the feminine ending (*ʾayyah*) is extremely frequent, and a more systematic concordance of gender

27. An important step towards a return to the linguistic habit of the *ʾiʿrāb* was the decree of the ministries of education of the U.A.R. and Morocco that, beginning in October of 1959, the textbooks of the primary and secondary schools would be vocalized. Both countries are also actively concerned with reforming the printed Arabic script. The Moroccan authorities have already endorsed a new plan of reform. When the Academy of the Arabic Language in Cairo opened an inquiry into this problem, it was confronted with no less than 280 new proposals for reform. See *Revista del Instituto de Estudios Islámicos en Madrid* 7–8 (Madrid, 1959–60): 174–76. The main proposals concerning the modification of the Arabic script have been discussed by the conference held by the Cairo Academy in January, 1944. See the texts of these proposals, together with the debates they provoked, in the Academy's publication *Majmaʿ Fuʾād al-ʾAwwal li al-Lughah al-ʿArabīyah: Muʾtamar al-Majmaʿ—Sanah 1944. Taysīr al-Kitābah al-ʿArabīyah* (Cairo, 1946).

28. Ḥasan al-Sharīf proposed that masculine-gender nouns admitting sound plurals should have such plurals only to the exclusion of all the possible broken ones. Substantives not admitting sound plurals would have only one broken plural form. See his article "*Tabsīṭ Qawāʿid al-Lughah al-ʿArabīyah,*" in *Al-Hilāl* (August 1938), pp. 1108–1119, and its discussion by Naffūsah Zakariyā Saʿīd in her *Taʾrīkh al-Daʿwah*, pp. 201–3.

29. H. Reckendorf, *Arabische Syntax* (Heidelberg, 1921), p. 148.

tends to become the normal usage in prose as well as in poetry. Thus we read in a poem by ʾAbū al-Qāsim al-Shābbī:

> *Naḥnu namshī . . . wa ḥawlanā hātihi al-ʾakwā*
> *nu tamshī . . . lākinna li ʾayyati ghāyah.*[30]

Or there is this example of a rather pedantic insistence upon the feminine concordance: *wa lākinnī ʿalā ʾayyati ḥālin qad intabahtu ʾilayhi.*[31] Or in the conversational style of a modern novel: *ʾAyyatu mufājaʾatin saʿīdatin baʿda dhālika al-taʾrīkhi al-ṭawīli!*[32]

Yet, the indiscriminate use of *ʾayy* and *ʾayyah* with nouns of feminine gender is still relatively frequent: *wa laysa ʿalayhā ʾasāsīyan ʾayyatu masʾūlīyatin mālīyatin wa ʾayyu nafaqātin maḥdūdatin.*[33]

A normalization of the grammatical gender of the noun *zawj*, which in classical Arabic means either husband or wife, is taking place in modern usage.[34] This process, too, like the one observed with regard to *ʾayy*, is but an accentuation of an incipient classical phenomenon. The Umayyad poet Dhū al-Rummah, for instance, uses *zawjah.*[35] The contemporary Egyptian novelist Najīb Maḥfūẓ, however, consistently uses *zawj* for both genders.

Among the more apparent new developments regarding the verb can be mentioned the change in the use of the sixth form of *saʾala* (to ask). Thus, *tasāʾala* is now frequently being used not in order to express the reciprocity of questioning, but rather with a reflexive meaning, instead of the expression *sāʾala nafsahu* (he asked himself, he directed to himself a question). More rigid philologists reject this use of *tasāʾala*, as, for example, Muṣṭafā Jawād, who reminds a certain writer that *al-tasāʾul* (mutual questioning) can exist among two persons at least.[36] On the

30. ʾAbū al-Qāsim al-Shābbī, *ʾAghānī al-Ḥayāh*, p. 141.
31. *Apollo* 2, no. 1:28.
32. Najīb Maḥfūẓ, *Al-Sukkarīyah*, p. 290.
33. *Apollo* 2, no. 2:152.
34. Monteil, *L'arabe moderne*, p. 127.
35. Murād Kāmil, *Dalālat al-ʾAlfāẓ al-ʿArabīyah wa Taṭawwuruhā* (Cairo, 1963), p. 41.
36. *Apollo* 2, no. 5:357.

whole, however, even prominent authors do not shun the reflexive use of *tasāʾala*, so that we read in ʾAnīs al-Khūrī al-Maqdisī *wa yaqifu . . . ḥāʾiran mutasāʾilan* (and he stops perplexed, asking himself);[37] or *thumma yatasāʾalu mutahakkiman* (then he asked himself ironically).[38] ʾAḥmad ʾAmīn, too, writes *wa yafriḍu al-furūḍa fa yatasāʾalu* (and he states the suppositions and asks himself).[39] Or ʿAbbās Maḥmūd al-ʿAqqād, speaking before the Academy of the Arabic Language, *wa ʾinnī la ʾatasāʾalu* (and I do ask myself).[40]

Similarly, the verb *talāʿaba* (to play with someone) is used with reference to one agent only, disregarding the etymological connotation of mutuality, as in the expression *wa yatalāʿabu (shāʿirun) bi ʾalfāẓihi* ([a poet] plays with his words).[41] The classical usage of *talāʿaba* implied reciprocity, as in *al-talāʿub bi al-silāḥ*, with reference to chivalrous, armed engagements or practices, and instead the Form V (*talaʿʿaba*) was used for the above modern meaning.[42]

Examples like these are so numerous that it is not easy to follow Muṣṭafā Jawād and speak of errors or ignorance of the language. One is rather inclined to accept these examples as new usages and as symptoms of a general flexibility, rather than laxity, in regard to traditional grammatical rules and linguistic habits.

There is a clear trend in modern Arabic towards a simplification and standardization of the gender agreement between verb and noun in sentences where the verb precedes the noun. A grammatically masculine noun produces a masculine gender agreement of the verb, and a feminine noun a corresponding feminine agreement. Masculine bro-

37. Al-Maqdisī, *Al-Ittijāhāt*, p. 388; see also p. 285.

38. Ibid., p. 284.

39. ʾAḥmad ʾAmīn, *Ḍuḥā al-ʾIslām*, 3:292.

40. *Majmaʿ al-Lughah al-ʿArabīyah—Majmūʿat al-Buḥūth wa al-Muḥāḍarāt*, (Cairo, 1960), 1:183.

41. Maḥmūd Muḥammad Sulaymān, in *Al-ʾAdīb*, year 24, no. 3 (March 1965), p. 10.

42. Mandūr, *Al-Naqd al-Manhajī*, p. 267, quotes from the *Yatīmat al-Dahr* by al-Thaʿālibī: *al-talaʿʿub bi al-kalām*, with the meaning of "playing with words" or, rather, "using words effectively."

ken plurals, too, agree in gender with preceding verbs. Thus, whereas a classical author writes *wa rubbamā taṭrabu ᵓilā ᵓaklihā al-mulūku* (and often kings are delighted to eat them),[43] a modern writer would almost invariably say *yaṭrabu . . . al-mulūku.*

The phenomenon of the *ᵓiqḥām,* which is the insertion into a "construct group" of another noun in the same case as the *muḍāf ᵓilayhi,* and connected to it by means of *wa,* has become now a regular stylistic feature. Its simplifying effect derives from the dispensation with the otherwise necessary pronoun of reference. Thus, *mudunu wa qurā Miṣra* would be used instead of the more classical *mudunu Miṣra wa qurāhā* (the towns and villages of Egypt). Hans Wehr thinks that the frequency of the *ᵓiqḥām* in modern Arabic may be due to the influence of European languages,[44] although it already appears in classical texts.

Burdensome repetition of prepositions within the same clause is frequently avoided, as in the following example from Najīb Maḥfūẓ: *wa lākin li tayaqquẓi al-shakki wa fiᶜlihi* (but because of the awakening of doubt and its effect).[45] Otherwise the clause would have ended *wa li fiᶜlihi.* This type of simplification is not entirely modern either. Only its frequency is characteristic of the modern style.

As a rule, classical usage accepts the putative *qad* with the imperfect in positive clauses only, since this *qad* should not be separated from its verb. Modern usage, however, admits the interposition of the negative particle *lā* between *qad* and the imperfect of a verb: *qad yakūnu* (he may be); *qad lā yakūnu* (he may not be). This spontaneous tendency towards standardization has been unsuccessfully criticized by the Cairo Academy.[46]

The conjunction *wa,* which commonly introduces the classical Arabic sentence, tends to be used in modern Arabic only where actual copulative clauses exist. No

43. ᵓAbū al-ᶜAlāᵓ al-Maᶜarrī, *Risālat al-Ghufrān,* p. 42.
44. Wehr, "Entwicklung und traditionelle Pflege," pp. 38–39.
45. Najīb Maḥfūẓ, *Zuqāq al-Midaqq,* p. 79.
46. *Majallat Majmaᶜ al-Lughah al-ᶜArabīyah al-Malakī,* 1:138.

longer is it customary to resort to it as a quasi punctuation device in a narrative sentence-sequence. The *al-wāw al-ḥālīyah* of the interpolated circumstantial clause may disappear too, allowing a more direct phrasing. Thus, Najīb Maḥfūẓ writes: *fa labitha yuḥamliqu fī al-ẓalmāʾi, fuʾāduhu khāfiqun* (he went on staring into the darkness, his heart throbbing).[47]

Further inquiry into modern Arabic linguistic usage is necessary. This would indicate the degree of urgency for a comprehensive study of modern Arabic syntax in particular.

47. Najīb Maḥfūẓ, *Zuqāq al-Midaqq*, p. 224.

Foreign Modes of Expression (*Taʿrīb al-ʾAsālīb*) 6

THE assimilation of foreign stylistic particularities is a process far from being confined exclusively to the present moment in the history of the Arabic language. The great body of non-Arabic vocabulary which has become arabicized even in pre-Islamic times suggests that there might and must have been more far-reaching changes in the language, transcending mere lexical assimilation. Yet, partly because of the barrier of time which separates us from the origins of recorded Arabic literature and partly because of insufficient study of Arabic stylistics, our knowledge of the evolution of the Arabic language is mostly limited to whatever information we possess about the influx of new vocabulary into the Arabic lexicon. Those changes, however, which imply turns of phrases, characteristic idiomatic expressions, and other stylistic particularities, still require a great amount of attention. Generally speaking, one should observe that the history of the Arabic language, and in a particular way the history of Arabic stylistic developments, is, if not entirely neglected, still a greatly unexploited field.

When we come to the early Abbasid period, we find that

a stylistic inquiry at that point could already become rewarding and conclusive. The new ranks of poets and writers, many of them *muwalladūn* and bilingual, bring into Arabic much that is inherent in their race and ancestral language. Here one can not avoid thinking of Ibn al-Muqaffaᶜ and of his contribution to Arabic prose. His style and the genres he introduced were soon imitated and developed. Particularly in the present literary revival, when there appeared the need to purify the language of all the debris left from centuries of decadence, Ibn al-Muqaffaᶜ was declared to be one of the ideal models for imitation—an exponent of old Arabic values in style and language: clarity, sobriety and purity. Yet Ibn al-Muqaffaᶜ was not of Arabic stock. His true tongue was not Arabic but Persian, and his language lacked one of those three ideal requirements mentioned above, which is purity in the Arabic sense. In his writings we find a number of Persian words, newly arabicized (probably by himself); his style, too, which does not flow quite naturally, appears to reveal a foreign hand. Ibn al-Muqaffaᶜ's stylistic particularities are not yet sufficiently established, however, to serve as a reliable yardstick for the study of Persian influence upon Arabic prose. From the Abbasid time onwards, Arabic styles tend to be ever more unified and imitative of each other. This presents remarkable difficulties for the classification of individual styles, although the general stratification into regions and epochs remains on the whole discernible.

Yet, it is not until the present *Nahḍah*-movement that we are in a position to register stylistic innovations and foreign influences as they find their way into the Arabic language. These foreign stylistic innovations, which sometimes influence the entire phrasing of a sentence, introduce hitherto unknown punctuation and even affect the basic structural idea of the Arabic sentence. Such innovations ought to be of the greatest concern to modern Arab linguists interested in the genesis and development of the modern Arabic literary language. Nevertheless, until now, relatively little has been done in this field.

This neglect is partly due to the resistance of conservative Arab littérateurs and philologists to any encroachment whatsoever upon the classical language. To study new linguistic phenomena objectively would mean to them a bestowal of legitimacy. A further reason for this neglect may be the gradual and imperceptible way in which these new stylistic developments occur, fostered by a new habit of bilingual thinking and by linguistic conditioning through translations. Thus there comes a point where Arabic takes over stylistic calques quite organically, with improvised variants of its own making, and where the Arab writer and reader fail to perceive the strangeness of the new expressions altogether. Consequently, the study of modern stylistic developments from within Arabic becomes increasingly difficult. A similar study carried on outside the language seems easier, at least in a gross, primary form. However, attempts of some significance by Arab philologists to study these phenomena have already been made. Three contributions in particular deserve to be mentioned: two of them for their chronologically pioneering positions (ᵓIbrāhīm al-Yāzijī's *Lughat al-Jarāᵓid* [1901] and Jurjī Zaydān's *Al-Lughah al-ᶜArabīyah Kāᵓin Ḥayy* (1904), specifically the chapter "Al-Tarākīb al-ᵓAᶜjamīyah"), and the third one for its solid and objective method (the Academy paper on *Taᶜrīb al-ᵓAsālīb* (1934), by ᶜAbd al-Qādir al-Maghribī).[1]

Al-Yāzijī's essay still falls short of being a methodical study of our precise subject. It is a listing of diverse semantic and stylistic irregularities in the modern journalistic language. The author's purpose is to purge rather than to record. The examples he quotes, however, constitute in themselves a valuable source, to which we shall turn occasionally.

Among the examples of non-Arabic stylistic innovations quoted by Jurjī Zaydān, the most outstanding are the following.

1. The paper was first published in the *Majallat Majmaᶜ Fuᵓād al-ᵓAwwal li al-Lughah al-ᶜArabīyah,* pt. 1, pp. 332 ff., and then incorporated into the second edition of al-Maghribī's *Kitāb al-Ishtiqāq wa al-Taᶜrīb;* see a further discussion of this topic by al-Maghribī and the Academy in *Minutes,* 1 (1934): 327–28.

Ra'aytu ṣadīqī (fulān) alladhī 'aʿṭānī al-kitāba. The correct Arabic expression would require *fa 'aʿṭānī al-kitāba,* the excessive use of the relative pronoun being one of the tendencies in modern Arabic.

Mustamiddan al-ʿināyata min al-Lāhi, 'aqifu baynakum khaṭīban. Here it is not only the choice of vocabulary which reveals a non-Arabic way of thought, but even more so the gerund structure of the sentence.

Yūjadu fī bilādi al-Ḥijāz ʿiddatu jibālin. The frequent use of *yūjadu* for "there is" is a modern development as well.

ʿAbd al-Qādir al-Maghribī's study of the subject is much more elaborate, and the term of *taʿrīb al-'asālīb,* which we have adopted, is actually his own.[2] To begin with, he states that those foreign stylistic modes which use purely Arabic vocabulary are not easily identifiable. In some cases there may be a natural coincidence between the way of expression in Arabic and a given foreign language. Elsewhere it will be the case that, although there might exist antecedents and analogical cases authentically Arabic, they had fallen into oblivion only to be reactivated under the influence of their foreign stylistic counterparts. The most numerous group of stylistic neologisms consists of expressions which have found their way into Arabic through translations from Western literatures and through the overall contact with Western cultural environments.

1. The first group of expressions studied by al-Maghribī includes those which reveal close parallelisms with expressions in other languages, without having been influenced by them:

ramā 'ākhira sahmin fī kinānatihi	(to fire one's last cartridge)
iftaḥ 'udhnayka	(*ouvres les oreilles*)
khānathu quwāhu	(*ses forces le trahirent*)
shariba al-ka'sa ḥattā al-thumāli	(*boire le calice jusqu'à la lie*)
fulānun dharibu al-lisāni	(*avoir la langue bien affilée*)

2. Al-Maghribī, *Al-Ishtiqāq,* p. 98.

2. Next are cases which can possibly be referred to expressions authentically Arabic, which, however, became abandoned in the course of time or were used in a different context.

Here the most interesting and the most controversial example is that of the auxiliary use of the verb *ʿāda—yaʿūdu* (to return) in negative expressions like *fulānun mā ʿāda yaqdiru ʾan yusāfira; fulānun mā ʿudtu raʾaytuhu; mā ʿāda (lam yaʿud) al-dahru yusʿifunā bi mithli fulānin; fulānun mā ʿāda ṣadīqan lī (lam yaʿud ṣadīqan lī).*[3]

The general notion is that this use of the verb *ʿāda* was introduced in the past century through translations from the French language. The translators found that in French there are two negative expressions: *ne pas* and *ne plus.* The expressions with *ne plus* were then translated by means of the verb *ʿāda.* Therefore, the difference between the two negative sentences *mā qadartu ʾan ʾarā Zaydan* and *mā ʿudtu ʾaqdiru ʾan ʾarā Zaydan* is like the difference between French sentences with *ne pas* and with *ne plus,* respectively. Thus the verb *ʿāda* with a negative particle acquires the secondary nature of an auxiliary verb. Of course, the auxiliary aspect of *ʿāda* is not new. It is evident in the Koran, in the *Ḥadīth,* and in other classical documents, but never appears in them used with a negative particle. A simple classical example of *ʿāda* as one of the *ʾakhawāt kāna* is *ʿudta ʿabdan* (you became a slave), or of its synonym *irtadda: irtadda baṣīran* (*er wurde wieder sehend*);[4] or in combination with another synonym (*ʿāda—ʾāḍa*): *La ʿāda dhālika kulluhu wa ghayruhu min al-muʿqayāti yuʿaddu min al-ladhāʾidhi al-murtaqayāti fa ʾāḍa mā kuriha min al-ṣābi kaʾannahu al-muʿtaṣaru min al-muṣābi.*[5]

When the auxiliary *ʿāda* is joined to another verb, this is done by means of the conjunction *fa,* as in *ʿudtu fa sharibtu* (I drank again). Such a use remained a very common stylistic practice even among the present modernists.

Making an effort at schematization, one may observe

3. See the entire discussion of this topic in ibid., pp. 102–3.
4. Reckendorf, *Arabische Syntax,* p. 100.
5. ʾAbū al-ʿAlāʾ al-Maʿarrī, *Risālat al-Ghufrān,* pp. 44–45.

within classical Arabic the following development taking place in the use of *ʿāda*. At an initial stage the verb experiences a general abstraction and semantic extension. This is evident in the koranic *thumma yaʿūdūna li mā qālū.*[6] The extended *ʿāda* can then function as an auxiliary verb, first with the conjunction and then without it. Thus we would get a schematic progression from *ʿāda li mā qāla* to *ʿāda fa qāla* to *ʿāda yaqūlu*. The progress is from an initial metaphoric abstract use to an idiomatic one, where the semantic switch from the concrete to the abstract is already fully automatic, and where, formally, the main verb (*yaqūlu*) becomes the circumstance (*ḥāl*).

Positive sentences with this extended or auxiliary *ʿāda* might, in theory, be converted into negative ones, even though there does not seem to be any purely classical evidence of such a usage. Thus, quoting from the *Ḥadīth*—*ʾa ʿudta fattānan yā Muʿādhu*—al-Maghribī asks himself: "And if Muʿādh had wanted to answer the Prophet, would he have said to him *lastu fattānan yā Rasūla al-Lāhi*, or rather *lam ʾaʿud fattānan*, by means of *ʿāda?*"[7] The answer to this question we shall never know, yet this allowed al-Maghribī to spell out the hypothesis that a limited use among the Arabs of the negative group *mā ʿāda* is a theoretical possibility, even though the current spread of it might be the work of modern translators.[8] As for the earliest notice taken of the group *mā ʿāda* in a lexicographical work, it occurs in the *Dictionnaire français-arabe*, by Ellious Bocthor, which was composed at a date prior to 1821 and published in 1828 under the direction of Armand Caussin de Perceval. This shows that a consistent use of this particular type of expression antedates the great wave of translations of French literature into Arabic.

In most recent writings, one can come upon further complications of the *ʿāda* group, as in: *wa taʿūdu al-mush-*

6. Koran, Sura LVIII, 4.

7. Al-Maghribī, *Al-Ishtiqāq*, p. 103.

8. The present author is confident of having come across *mā ʿāda* group expressions in pre-*Nahḍah* writings. Some instances, however, like that attributed to Ibn Mammātī, in *Al-Hilāl* (year 74, no. 8, p. 100), appear to be modern paraphrases.

kilatu al-siyāsīyatu li taṭfuwa ʿalā al-saṭḥi (the political problem comes to the surface once again),[9] where the preposition introducing the meaning-carrying verb may be viewed as an irregularity.[10]

Among other expressions about whose non-Arabic origin there may be reasonable doubt, al-Maghribī includes the use of the verb *tabādala* (to exchange): *tabādalā al-taḥīyāti; tabādalā baʿḍa al-kalimāti;* and so on. The only problem here is that in classical Arabic the use of this verb is limited to material objects (*tabādalā thawbayhimā*), whereas in European languages and in contemporary Arabic it can also be used where abstract concepts are concerned. For this abstract use the Arabs had the verb *taqāraḍa* (*taqāraḍā al-ziyārata*).

A very similar case is that of the expression *raghma* or *bi raghmi* (in spite). The modern use, most probably under Western influence, permits expressions like *sa ʾusāfiru ghadan bi raghmi al-maṭari* or *bi raghmin min al-maṭari* (in spite of the rain), whereas in classical Arabic such reference can be made to a person only (*bi raghmī; ʿalā raghmi ʾanfihi; raghma ʾanfi fulānin*, and so on).

In the same category of doubtful authenticity, yet not clearly non-Arabic, al-Maghribī includes expressions like *wa bi al-naẓari ʾilā* (in regard to); *wa fī al-waqti nafsihi jāʾa fulānun* (at the same time); *fulānun yaʿmalu ḍidda fulānin* (to act against); *qatala al-waqta* (to kill time); *hādhihi masʾalatun jawharīyatun* (this is an essential question); *al-ʾamru kadhā* (the matter is like this) *wa bi ʿibāratin ʾawḍaḥa ʾaw bi ʿibāratin ʾaṣaḥḥa* (and more properly speaking) *huwa kadhā wa kadhā* (it is so-and-so).[11]

9. ʿAbd al-Muḥsin Ṭaha Badr, *Taṭawwur al-Riwāyah,* p. 38.

10. Compare, however, with such classical examples as *mā kāna huwa li yaḍurranā* (he is not [the man] to do us any harm); *mā kāna al-Lāhu li yuḍīʿa ʾīmānakum* (God is incapable of letting [lit., is not (the one) to let] your belief perish). See Wright: *Grammar of the Arabic Language,* 2:266.

11. It is difficult to understand, however, how al-Maghribī could have had any doubts about the non-authenticity, from the Arabic point of view, of expressions like *fulānun yumaththilu al-majmaʿa fī al-ḥaflati al-rasmīyah,* where, except for *fulān,* practically every word is in a sense a modern derivation; or *jawwu al-siyāsati mukahrabun!*

3. Finally, there is the category of expressions unquestionably non-Arabic:[12] *ʾazhara al-ʿumrānu; ʾazharat al-maʿrifatu; izdaharat al-tijāratu* (to flourish, as of civilization, knowledge, commerce); *sāda al-jahlu; sādat al-fawḍā* (to reign, as of ignorance, anarchy);[13] *fulānun yuʾayyiduhu al-raʾyu al-ʿāmmu* (somebody supported by public opinion); *wa ʾaqūlu ʾanā fī dawrī* (*à mon tour*); *faʿala kadhā bi ṣifatihi ḥākiman li al-bilādi* or *fulānun faʿala kadhā . . . ka muʾarrikhin* (*en qualité de, comme un*);[14] *masʾalatun basīṭatun; rajulun basīṭun; qāla dhālika bi basāṭatin* (a simple problem, a simple man, he said it with simplicity); *tarjamatun saṭḥīyatun; maʿrifatun saṭḥīyatun; baḥthun saṭḥīyun* (superficial); *kānat al-ḥaflatu taḥta ʾishrāfi fulānin ʾaw taḥta riʿāyati maʿālī al-wazīri* (*sous les auspices*); *fulānun laʿiba dawran ʾaw maththala dawran fī hādhihi al-qaḍīyati* (to play a role).

These were some of the newly arabicized expressions pointed out by al-Maghribī. Their frequency in contemporary prose is extremely high, and even the poetic language has begun to be affected by them. The smoothness with which the last example (*laʿiba dawran*) was assimilated into poetic language can be appreciated in the beautiful short poem by ʾAbū al-Qāsim al-Shābbī, entitled "Al-Riwāyah al-Gharībah."[15]

Aside from, or rather parallel to, the classification pursued by ʿAbd al-Qādir al-Maghribī—a classification where the point of reference is the classical language, and where the stylistic borrowings form three categories according to their respective approximation to or deviation from the classical stylistic molds—a series of mostly new examples of stylistic borrowings will be given, grouped

12. Al-Maghribī (*Al-Ishtiqāq*, pp. 107–110) quotes more than thirty such expressions.

13. In classical Arabic, *siyādah* can be attributed to persons only.

14. In classifying an expression like *ka muʾarrikhin* as clearly non-Arabic, al-Maghribī evidently had not taken into consideration Abbasid prose. Here we have a question of frequency and not of innovation.

15. ʾAbū al-Qāsim al-Shābbī, *ʾAghānī al-Ḥayāh*, p. 146. See in the same poem such expressions as *masraḥu al-ḥayāti, masraḥu al-ʿālami al-kabīru*, and others.

into four categories, with reference to syntax, lexicon, and idiomatic topicality:

1. stylistic borrowings affecting syntactic structure
2. literal translations from Western languages with eventual disregard of existing Arabic equivalents
3. stylistic borrowings made possible through semantic extension and abstraction
4. assimilation of proverbial and idiomatic expressions

1. Stylistic borrowings affecting syntactic structure.

ʿAbathan ʾantaẓiru al-ʾāna fa najmī laysa yaṭlaʿu (In vain do I wait).[16]

ʾInna al-ḥayāta lā wa lan tuḥāwila tabriʾata nafsihā ʾamāma al-mawti wa al-ḥaqīqatu lā wa lan tashraḥa dhātahā (Life does not and will not justify itself, and truth does not and will not explain itself).[17]

Wa ʾazʿumu ʾannahu lam wa lan yafhama min muqaddimatihi shayʾan (He did not and he will not understand).[18] Notice in both above examples the reference of two diversely governing negative particles to only one verb.

Wa sawfa tajidu wasīlatan ʾaw ʾukhrā li al-ittiṣāli bi Karīmah (You will find one means or another to get in touch with K.)[19] Here *ʾukhrā* replaces more cumbersome constructions with a pronoun of reference or with the partitive *min*.

ʾInnī shākiratun laka hādhā, wa lākin laysa "ʾanā" al-ladhī ʾamliku al-radda ʿalayhi (I am thankful to you for this, but it is not in *my* means to reciprocate).[20] The verbal use of *shākiratun* is in this case a rendering of "I am thankful," made easy by the colloquial preference for the participle. The author of this line was himself uncomfortable

16. Nāzik al-Malāʾikah *ʿĀshiqat al-Layl*, p. 42. Compare with the expression *mustamiddan al-ʿināyata min al-Lāhi ʾaqifu baynakum khaṭīban* (above, p. 98).

17. Muḥyī al-Dīn Riḍā, ed., *Balāghat al-ʿArab fī al-Qarn al-ʿIshrīn* (Cairo, 1924), p. 56 (from Jubrān Khalīl Jubrān).

18. Ṭaha Ḥusayn, *Ḥadīth al-ʾArbaʿāʾ*, 3:101.

19. Najīb Maḥfūẓ, *Al-Ṭarīq*, p. 151.

20. Najīb Maḥfūẓ, *Bidāyah wa Nihāyah* (Cairo, 1958), p. 90.

with the use of *ʾanā* after *laysa*, followed by a verb in the first person (compare with *lastu ʾamliku*).

Wa kullu ḥubbin, likay yakūna mawḍūʿa al-shiʿri, yajibu ʾan yakūna al-fidāʾa wa al-khalāṣa maʿan (All love, in order to be the subject of poetry, ought to be both redemption and salvation).[21] Even though complex sentences with interpolated clauses are common in high Abbasid prose, the modern predilection for interpolation goes beyond classical limits, like this introduction of the secondary clause with *likay* in the middle rather than at the end of the sentence.

ʾIbrāhīm al-Yāzijī had already observed in *Lughat al-Jarāʾid* that the tendency to use the conditional *ʾin* and the temporal *ʾidhā* with the meaning of "whether" was a result of literal rendering of Western stylistic models. Thus: *unẓur ʾin kāna Zaydun fī dārihi wa salhu ʾidhā kāna al-ʾamru kadhā* (Look whether Zayd is at home and ask him whether the matter is so-and-so!).[22] Hans Wehr remarks that not only *ʾin* and *ʾidhā* but also *law* may now introduce indirect interrogative sentences. Thus: *saʾalahā al-qāḍī ʿan ismihā wa sinnihā wa ʿammā law kānat irtakabat al-jarīmata* (. . . and whether she had committed the crime).[23] Considering that classical Arabic had no distinctive way of expressing an indirect question, these modern usages ought to be regarded as a formal syntactical innovation.

In the majority of cases the quasi interrogative *ʾin* is introduced by the verb *darā* (to know): *lā yadrī ʾin . . . ʾam* (not to know whether . . . or).[24]

Examining the style of the contemporary Egyptian novelist Najīb Maḥfūẓ, we may observe a trend towards normalization with regard to this nonclassical use of *ʾin*.

21. *Shiʿr* (review) 6, no. 22 (Spring 1962): 110.

22. ʾIbrāhīm al-Yāzijī, *Lughat al-Jarāʾid*, p. 34.

23. According to Hans Wehr, however, such a use of *ʾin* must not necessarily derive from the French *si*. He finds similar usages in al-Ghazālī already. See his *Die Besonderheiten des heutigen Hocharabischen*, p. 62.

24. For further discussion of this usage see *Minutes*, 1 (1934): 160–162 (by ʾAḥmad al-ʿAwāmirī); also Monteil, *L'arabe moderne*, pp. 245–46.

Whereas in his early writings this usage is still an exception to the rule, in his later books, approximately beginning with the Trilogy, it becomes the rule. In *Zuqāq al-Midaqq* (1947) we normally encounter expressions like *fa lam tadri ʾa ʾaṣābat ʾam ʾakhṭaʾat fī* . . . (she did not know whether she was right or wrong about . . .);[25] from *Bayna al-Qaṣrayn* (1956) on, however, expressions of the *ʾin* variety predominate. The following are some of these expressions.

Wa lammā ʾāwat ʾilā ḥujratihā lam tadri ʾin kānat tawaddu—kamā daʿat bi lisānihā ʾamāma ʾabnāʾihā—ʾan yastura al-Lāhu ʿalā jināyati Yāsīn ʾam ʾannahā tarjū ʾan yanāla ʾaw bi al-ʾaḥrā ʾan tanāla zawjuhu jazāʾahā min al-zajri wa al-taʾdībi? (. . . she did not know whether she liked . . . God to cover up Yāsīn's crime or rather that . . .).[26]

Yanbaghī ʾan ʾaʿrifa ʾawwalan ʾin kuntu saʾabqā fī Miṣra ʾam lā (First I have to know whether I shall stay in Egypt or not).[27]

Bal lā ʾadrī ʾin kuntu ʾuḥibbuhā ʾin wujidat (Besides, I don't know whether I would love her if she existed).[28]

Hādhihi al-marrata lā nadrī ʾin kunnā sa narā Miṣra karratan ʾukhrā ʾam lā (This time we don't know whether we would have seen Egypt once more or not).[29]

ʿAbd al-Munʿim sa yatazawwaju ʾin al-yawma ʾam ghadan (ʿAbd al-Munʿim will marry—either today or tomorrow).[30]

2. Literal translations from European languages with eventual disregard of existing Arabic equivalents.

Fulānun ṭalāba yada fulānatin (X asked for the hand of Y).[31] The Arabic equivalent (*khaṭabahā*) tends to be disregarded by modern prose writers. In this borrowing

25. Najīb Maḥfūẓ, *Zuqāq al-Midaqq*, p. 83.

26. Najīb Maḥfūẓ, *Bayna al-Qaṣrayn*, p. 276. The constrained syntax of the rest of the sentence invites separate criticism.

27. Najīb Maḥfūẓ: *Qaṣr al-Shawq*, p. 249.

28. Ibid., p. 352.

29. Najīb Maḥfūẓ, *Al-Sukkarīyah*, p. 176.

30. Ibid., p. 223. Here *ʾin* stands for "either" only because of an implicit *lā ʾadrī* separating it from the main clause.

31. *Minutes*, 1 (1934):328.

Arabic has not yet neutralized the metaphoric nature of the denoted situation.

Fulānun qaraʾa Fīktūr Hūjū (X read Victor Hugo).[32] Classical usage would not allow the omission of the concrete object (*al-kitāba*) in favor of the metaphoric one (Victor Hugo).

ʾAdāʾu wājibi al-zakāti naḥwahu—"Duty towards" is a borrowing.[33]

Laysa ladayhim ʾayyatu fikratin ʿan al-ḥayāti al-niyābīyati (They had no idea . . .).[34]

ʾAnta lam taʿrif maʿnā ʾan yakūna li ʾummika zawjun ghayru ʾabīka (It did not make any sense to you . . .).[35]

Fī al-maqāmi al-ʾawwali (In the first place).[36]

ʾAnā madyūnun li fulānin fī hādhā al-ʾamri (I am indebted to . . .).[37] The equivalent classical expression would be *lahu ʿalayya faḍlun fī*.

Thalāthatun ʿalā al-ʾaqalli min ʾaʿḍāʾi al-majmaʿi (at least).[38] ʾAnastās al-Kirmalī protested against this use of *ʿalā al-ʾaqalli*, suggesting instead *lā ʾaqalla min thalāthatin*.[39]

Raʾaytuhu ʾakthara min marratin (more than once).

Jāʾanī ʾaktharu min wāḥidin (more than one). ʾIbrāhīm al-Yāzijī recommends, instead, *raʾaytuhu ghayra marratin* and *jāʾanī ghayru wāḥidin*.[40]

A related usage is the adverbial *ʾakthara fa ʾakthara* (more and more): *hādhihi al-kalimatu allatī tanʿatu ʾakthara fa ʾakthara jamīʿa wujūhi al-ḥayāti*.[41] A similar use of reiterated comparatives is common in classical Arabic, however.

32. Ibid., 1:328.
33. *Apollo* 1, no. 1:4–5.
34. ʿAbd al-Muḥsin Ṭaha Badr, *Taṭawwur al-Riwāyah*, p. 25.
35. Najīb Maḥfūẓ, *Al-Sukkarīyah*, p. 60.
36. ʿAbd al-Muḥsin Ṭaha Badr, *Taṭawwur al-Riwāyah*, p. 29.
37. ʾIbrāhīm al-Yāzijī, *Lughat al-Jarāʾid*, pp. 62–63.
38. *Minutes*, 1:30.
39. Ibid., p. 31.
40. ʾIbrāhīm al-Yāzijī, *Lughat al-Jarāʾid*, pp. 49–50. Being a careful stylist, Ṭaha Ḥusayn, for example, avoids this use of *ʾakthara* in an elegant classical way: *yuqallidu al-Mutanabbī wāḥidan ʾaw ghayra wāḥidin min alladhīna sabaqūhu* (*Maʿa al-Mutanabbī* [Cairo, 1957], p. 36).
41. Thus Yūsuf al-Khāl, in *ʾAdab* 2, no. 1 (Winter 1963):9.

Notice even the more daring use al-Buḥturī makes of it in his *Sīnīyah:*

Kaʾanna al-zamāna ʾaṣbaḥa maḥmū—
lan hawāhu maʿa al-ʾakhassi al-ʾakhassi.

In expressions like *ʾahammu kathīran.* (much more important than . . .)[42] modern usage has adopted a qualitative meaning of *kathīran*, which actually corresponds to *jiddan.*

Fa huwa ghanīyun lā yaḥtāju ʾan yaksiba ḥayātahu (To earn one's living).[43]

ʿAbd al-Qādir al-Maghribī calls our attention to Ṭaha Ḥusayn's characteristic predilection for the following direct translations from the French:

khaṣṣaṣa ʿumrahu li al-ʾadabi wa li al-ʾadabi waḥdahu (*il a dédié sa vie à la littérature et rien qu'à la littérature*);

fakkartu ṭawīlan wa ṭawīlan jiddan (*j'ai réfléchi longtemps et bien longtemps*);

kāna al-qawmu mutaḥammisīna wa mutaḥammisīna jiddan (. . . *enthousiasmé, fortement enthousiasmé*);

wa huwa kathīrun wa kathīrun jiddan (. . . *trop, beaucoup trop*).[44]

Writers like Muḥammad Mandūr who either follow Ṭaha Ḥusayn's style or are directly influenced by the French language frequently use this construction as well: *ʾidhā kāna shiʿruhum lā yakhlū min saqaṭin wa saqaṭin kathīrin* (. . . not at all void of rubbish).[45]

42. Najīb Maḥfūẓ, *Zuqāq al-Midaqq*, p. 145.

43. Pierre Cachia, *Taha Husayn, His Place in the Egyptian Literary Renaissance* (London, 1956), p. 222.

44. Al-Maghribī, *Al-Ishtiqāq*, p. 110.

45. Mandūr, *Al-Naqd al-Manhajī*, p. 237. Even though al-Maghribī is right in identifying the above-mentioned expressions as being of French origin, there is an obvious stylistic affinity between these emphatic reiterations and another type of emphatic sentence, where the stress is even stronger, and where *jiddan*, etc. is replaced by *kull*, as in *wa qad ʾutīḥa lahu al-najāḥu kullu al-najāḥi fī mā ʿakafa ʿalayhi min al-darsi* (Ṭaha Ḥusayn in the Introduction to Ḥasan Ḥusayn Fahmī's *Al-Marjiʿ*, p. *ʾalif.*). This use of *kull*, however, is perfectly classical, as in this verse attributed to ʿAbd al-Raḥmān al-Dākhil:

Al-ḥazmu kullu al-ḥazmi ʾan lā yaghfulū
ʾa yarūmu tadbīra al-barrīyati ghāfilu.

The frequent modern use of this emphatic type of sentence, particu-

Yaqūlu al-Firansīyūna wa yuḥsinūna ᶜindamā yaqūlūna (The French say rightly).[46] Here only the use of *ᶜindamā* indicates a foreign influence. Notice, otherwise, the parallel with the Spanish idiom: *dice fulano, y dice bien.*

Hā huwa al-haramu yalūḥu min baᶜīdin ṣaghīran, wa ᶜammā qalīlin taqifu ᶜinda qadamayhi (. . . and soon you will stand at its foot).[47]

Ibtasama kaᵓannamā li yudāriya ḥayāᵓahu, wa lam yakun thammata ḥayāᵓun wa lākinnahu shaᶜara bi ᵓannahu "waqaᶜa" (. . . he felt that he had fallen: into the trap).[48] The author's own quotation marks indicate consciousness of an idiomatic use of *waqaᶜa.* Although we may think here of the French idiomatic *tomber*, this particular usage may also derive from an existing Egyptian colloquialism.

Wa ᵓimmā li ᵓannahu bāta yarā fī ṣāḥibihi mushākithan muḥtarifan (Or because he came to see in his friend a *professional* ruffian).[49] Notice the influence of an apparent English idiomatic usage.

Al-lamasātu al-khitāmīyah (Final touches).[50] The English model is apparent here as well.

ᵓArjū ᵓan takūna rajulan ᶜamalīyan (I wish you were a practical man).[51]

3. Stylistic borrowings made possible through semantic extension and abstraction.

Probably the largest number of arabicized expressions could be classified under this category. Many examples listed in the other categories could be included here as well.

---

larly by Ṭaha Ḥusayn, would indicate that the Arab writer's stylistic sensibility had already been conditioned and made receptive by analogical Arabic stylistic possibilities.

46. Salāmah Mūsā, *Al-ᵓAdab li ᵓal-Shaᶜb* (Cairo, 1956), p. 30.

47. Najīb Maḥfūẓ, *Qaṣr al-Shawq*, p. 170. Aside from the awkward dual, for a similar meaning Arabic has different words, like *safḥ* or *ḥaḍīḍ*, and Najīb Maḥfūẓ actually turns to the proper term later on the same page: *waqafat al-sayyāratu ghayra baᶜīdin min safḥi al-harami al-ᵓakbari.*

48. Najīb Maḥfūẓ, *Al-Sukkarīyah*, p. 154.

49. Najīb Maḥfūẓ, *Qaṣr al-Shawq*, p. 140.

50. Najīb Maḥfūẓ, *Al-Sarāb*, p. 87.

51. Najīb Maḥfūẓ, *Al-Qāhirah al-Jadīdah* (Cairo, 1958), p. 84.

The governing principle of the present group is always a semantically extended key element in a given sentence. This element, carrying either a metaphoric image or a semantic broadening through abstraction, may be a verb, a noun, or an adjective.

Out of a vast number of possible illustrations, only a representative few will be cited here.

Wa yaltamisu nafsahu, kamā yaqūlu al-Firansīyūna, fī hādhā al-taqlīdi (He tries to find himself, as the French say, within this tradition).[52] Here the Arab writer still reminds the reader that the phrase *yaltamisu nafsahu* is taken from the French language. Such reminders are rare, however, for most modern Arab writers tend to assimilate similar expressions with a matter-of-fact attitude.

Wa maqāmatu al-taᶜbīri hiya allatī tumlī ᶜalā al-ʾadībi istiᶜmāla hādhā al-lafẓi (It is the context which dictates to the writer the use of this word).[53] The new, extended meaning of *ʾamlā* can now take upon itself an abstract agent.

Wa ʾidhā shaᶜarū ʾanna hādhā al-ʾadaba al-jadīda yastaʾnifu ʾilā ᶜuqūlihim wa qulūbihim.[54] "To appeal to some one's mind and heart" constitutes the fullest semantic tension of a formerly legal term.

Al-ʾadību alladhī yansakhu ᶜan al-ṭabīᶜati (The writer who copies from nature).[55] The semantic extension of the verb is made possible by an initial metaphoric extension of "nature."

Wa ḍaḥḥat al-lughatu bi al-farqi bayna al-ʾajnāsi al-naḥwīyati (To sacrifice the difference).[56] In classical Arabic, *ḍaḥḥā bi* refers to concrete objects.

ʾInnahu yukarrisu waqtahu kullahu li al-mudhākarati (He dedicates his entire time to studying).[57] The etymology of the verb *karrasa* is concrete, leading back to a spe-

52. Ṭaha Ḥusayn, *Maᶜa al-Mutanabbī*, p. 36.

53. ᶜAbd al-Wahhāb Ḥammūdah, *Al-Tajdīd fī al-ʾAdab al-Miṣrī al-Ḥadīth* (Cairo: Dār al-Fikr al-ᶜArabī, n.d.), p. 67.

54. ʾAnīs Furayḥah, *Naḥwa ᶜArabīyatin Muyassarah*, p. 196.

55. Mārūn ᶜAbbūd, in a periodical article.

56. Murād Kāmil, *Dalālāt al-ʾAlfāẓ wa Taṭawwuruhā*, p. 38.

57. Najīb Maḥfūẓ, *Qaṣr al-Shawq*, p. 67; see also p. 349.

cific building material and to the act of firm construction.

Al-ḥallu alladhī tubashshiru bihi (The solution you preach).[58] The present semantic scope is fully comparable to that of the English "to preach."

Kamā yaqaᶜu li al-ᵓinsāni ᵓaḥyānan ᵓan yakhluqa mushkilatan wahmīyatan (As at times it happens to a person that he creates an imaginary problem).[59] The above use of *waqaᶜa* is not entirely modern. Its extended meaning may also be due to the influence of a colloquial association.

Wa rāḥat taltahimu al-makāna bi ᵓaᶜyunin shayyiqatin mustaṭliᶜatin (She devoured the place with eager, inquisitive eyes).[60] Aside from the verbal metaphoric extension, notice also the plural *ᵓaᶜyun* instead of a dual. This generic use of the plural, which should also be considered as a calque, is relatively frequent in modern Arabic.

Wa sāda ṣamtun mashḥūnun bi al-tawatturi ka al-ṣamti alladhī yarkabu ᵓaṭfālan fī al-ẓalāmi (There reigned a silence charged with tension, the kind of silence which overcomes children in the dark).[61] The semantic changes or extensions in this sentence range from classical (*yarkabu ᵓaṭfālan*), to postclassical (*mashḥūnun*), to modern (*sāda ṣamtun* and *al-tawattur*). The prevalent character of the entire sentence, however, is clearly modern.

Wa ḥaraṣa li dhālika ᶜalā ᵓan tughaṭṭiya riwāyatuhu kulla marāḥili al-taᵓrīkhi al-ᶜarabī (Because of that he wished that his novel would cover all the phases of Arab history).[62] Such an extension of the concrete meaning of *ghaṭṭā*, although a product of direct translation, follows the analogy of such classical extensions as *ᵓaḥāṭa*.

Qad tabalwarat fī shiᶜrihi ᵓāmālu ᵓummatihi (The hopes of his nation had crystallized in his poetry).[63] Being other-

58. Najīb Maḥfūẓ, *Bayna al-Qaṣrayn*, p. 298.

59. Ibid., p. 172.

60. Ibid., p. 150.

61. Ibid., p. 162. Frequently occurring modern expressions like *mashḥūnun bi al-kahrabāᵓi* (charged with electricity), or *mashḥūnun bi nashāṭin* (charged with energy), are only making use of the much earlier extended meaning of *shaḥana*.

62. ᶜAbd al-Muḥsin Ṭaha Badr, *Taṭawwur al-Riwāyah*, p. 95; another example from the same page: *li yughaṭṭiya hādhā al-imtidāda*.

63. ᶜAbd al-Wahhāb Ḥammūdah, *Al-Tajdīd fī al-ᵓAdab*, p. 117.

wise a neologism, the verb evolves in usage from concrete to abstract.

Yuwazziᶜu al-ᶜAqqādu al-būsa bi lā ḥisābin (Al-ᶜAqqād distributes [*répart*] kisses indiscriminately).[64] Here a colloquial influence has to be distinguished as well.

Kāna shabaḥu firāqik yuṭāridunī wa yuqiḍḍu maḍjaᶜī (The phantom of your departure was haunting me and depriving me of sleep).[65] Even though we may be tempted to accept this expression as basically modern, although with an interesting stylistic blending of old and new (notice *yuqiḍḍu maḍjaᶜī*), a closer examination of its language and image will send us back to the verse by al-Shanfarā (*Lāmīyat al-ᶜArab*):

> *Ṭarīdu jināyātin tayāsarna laḥmahu*
> *ᶜaqīratuhu li ʾayyihā ḥumma ʾawwalu.*

ᶜĀmat hādhihi al-khawāṭiru ᶜalā saṭḥi mukhkhihi ka al-faqāqīᶜi (These thoughts floated on the surface of his mind like bubbles).[66] Notice both *ᶜāmat al-khawāṭiru* and *ᶜalā saṭḥi mukhkhihi*. An otherwise more convenient verb than *ᶜāma* would be *ṭafā*.

Hākadhā saraḥat maᶜa ʾafkārihā al-wardīyati (Thus her rosy thought roamed freely).[67]

Thumma ibtasamat ʾilayya ibtisāmatan ṣafrāʾa (A pale smile).[68]

Māʾidatun shāghiratun (Gapingly empty table).[69]

Fī maylihā ʾilā al-ḥulīyi tabadhdhulun malmūsun (Tangible vulgarity).[70]

4. Borrowed proverbial and idiomatic expressions.

Calques within this category are relatively less numerous. They are also the most conspicuous and easily detectable.

64. Mārūn ᶜAbbūd, *ᶜAlā al-Miḥakk* (Beirut, 1946), p. 257.
65. Najīb Maḥfūẓ, *Al-Sarāb*, p. 112.
66. Najīb Maḥfūẓ, *Bayna al-Qaṣrayn*, p. 245.
67. Najīb Maḥfūẓ, *Zuqāq al-Midaqq*, p. 120.
68. Muḥammad ᶜAbd al-Ḥalīm ᶜAbd al-Lāh, *Shams al-Kharīf* (Cairo, n.d.), p. 9.
69. Najīb Maḥfūẓ, *Zuqāq al-Midaqq*, 247.
70. Ibid., p. 253.

ʾInnahu la yuḥriqu al-sufuna min warāʾihi (Burning one's boats).[71]

Fa kānat malakīyatan ʾakthara min al-maliki, kamā yuqālu (More royalist than the king).

Yanshurūna min hādhā al-qaṣaṣi alladhī lā raʾsa lahu wa lā dhayla (Story which has neither head nor tail).

Lā yastaṭīʿu ʾillā ʾan yarfaʿa qubbaʿatahu ʾijlālan li (To raise one's hat respectfully).[72]

Wa waḍaʿtuhā (al-masraḥīyata) fī durji maktabī (To put —a play—in the drawer).[73]

Wa kullila masʿāhum bi al-najāḥi (Their effort was crowned with success).[74]

Muzriyan bi kulli waṣfin (Mocking all description).[75]

Wa tamnaḥuhu al-lamasāti al-khitāmīyata (Giving it the finishing touches).[76]

Wa ʾakhīran wa laysa ʾākhiran (Last but not least).[77]

Fa shayʾun khayrun min lāshayʾin (Something is better than nothing).[78]

ʾUmūrukum al-ʿājilatu (Your urgent affairs).[79]

Qatlu al-waqti (Killing time).[80]

Sa naḍaʿuhu ʾamāma al-ʾamri al-wāqiʿi (*Nous allons le mettre devant le fait accompli*).[81] Whereas *al-ʾamr al-wāqiʿ* is clearly a calque, *sa naḍaʿuhu ʾamāma* may be misleading. A contemporary writer's expression like *ḍaʿū ʾanfusakum fī makānī* (put yourselves into my place),[82] even

71. Cachia, *Taha Husayn*, p. 222. This and the following two examples come from the pen of the French-educated Ṭaha Ḥusayn.

72. ʾAnīs Furayḥah, *Naḥwa ʿArabīyatin Muyassarah*, p. 13.

73. ʾAnwar al-Jundī, *Nazaʿāt al-Tajdīd* (Cairo, 1957), p. 158.

74. Najīb Maḥfūẓ, *Al-Sarāb*, p. 13.

75. Najīb Maḥfūẓ, *Qaṣr al-Shawq*, p. 16.

76. Najīb Maḥfūẓ, *Al-Sarāb*, p. 87.

77. Najīb Maḥfūẓ, *Zuqāq al-Midaqq*, p. 131.

78. Najīb Maḥfūẓ, *Al-Qāhirah al-Jadīdah*, p. 28.

79. Najīb Maḥfūẓ, *Zuqāq al-Midaqq*, p. 149.

80. ʾIbrāhīm al-Sāmarrāʾī registers the use of this idiom even in the language of the poet ʾAḥmad al-Ṣāfī al-Najafī and observes that, even though current in colloquial usage, it is originally a translation. See his *Lughat al-Shiʿr bayna Jīlayn*, p. 95.

81. *Al-ʾUsbūʿ al-ʿArabī*, no. 382, (30 October 1966), p. 44.

82. Najīb Maḥfūẓ, *Al-Sarāb*, p. 136.

though sounding borrowed, derives rather from al-Jāḥiẓ: *yaḍaʿu nafsahu fī mawḍiʿi al-ruqabāʾi.*[83]

What has already been said concerning the existence of semantic extension in Arabic should be repeated here. Not all conspicuously Western proverbial or idiomatic expressions are necessarily Western or modern. For instance, *ʾaṣghaytu ʾilayhā wa kullī ʾādhānun,* coming from Najīb Maḥfūẓ (*Al-Sarāb,* p. 271), is not a translated English idiom (I was all ears), but an echo of Ibn al-Fāriḍ's

ʾIdhā mā badat Laylā fa kulliya ʾaʿyunun
wa ʾin hiya nājatnī fa kullī masāmiʿu.[84]

Sometimes only a clear reference or the original context will tell us that a given expression is not a modern calque, as when the classical critic al-ʾĀmidī says: *mā huwa ʾillā ṣūratun fī al-ḥāʾiṭi* (it is but a picture on the wall).[85]

83. Al-Jāḥiẓ, *Rasāʾil al-Jāḥiẓ,* 1:6.
84. Ibn al-Fāriḍ, *Dīwān* (Beirut, 1962), p. 211.
85. As quoted by Muḥammad Mandūr in his *Al-Naqd al-Manhajī ʿinda al-ʿArab,* p. 313.

Definitions and Projections

As the reader must have noticed, the examples illustrating the preceding chapter operate by and large with a seemingly classical vocabulary. The illusion of having to do with unadulterated Arabic is there. The dictionary will only rarely be of any use in detecting deviations from the classical language. The occurring verbal semantic extensions are so broad and transparent that they do not impede satisfactory comprehension. Adjectival extensions have the backing of metaphorical context. The overall impression is that such a language is clear, precise, and self-explanatory. Writers and poets do not hesitate to use it. Critics rarely dwell on its particularity. In fact, the growing impression is that there does not seem to be attached to it any particularity any longer. It is not the "language of the journalists," as it used to be termed fifty years ago. Neither is it that of daring innovators or trend-setters. The air of inconspicuous anonymity and natural self-evidence has engulfed the stylistically borrowed idiom, which hardly anybody now perceives as extraneous to the tradition of the *al-fuṣḥā*. At the same time very few users of this new Arabic literary idiom realize how close it has brought them to other linguistic spheres. Translators can now quite effortlessly and smoothly render contemporary Arabic into other modern languages, and vice versa. Linguistic affinity is appearing where before there had only been disparity. Arabs find foreign languages easier—as others find Arabic.

Now that the stumbling block of a lack of semantic equivalence between the Arabic lexicon and the lexica of modern European languages has been largely overcome, the vocabulary question loses its forbidding character as a defining factor of the Arabic language. As for morphology, it has never been an insurmountable barrier between languages. It provides the pieces, the working elements of the verbal mosaic. It constitutes the elementary level of linguistic structure and logic, a level which varies little from one language to another—just as one elementary thought-formation varies little from another. Arabic is not different from English because *yaktubu* has a preformative and "writes" does not. The semantic and morphological logic is still the same. The simplest workable idea of an action has been conveyed in both cases. The shortest answer to the question "What does he do?" will be "write," "walk," and the like. An answer in Arabic might show some discrepancy, since *yaktubu* or *yamshī* reveal a different person. This is not so, however, because in the English case the full answer is either "he *does* write" or "he writes." A parallel with Spanish would be much closer: *¿Qué hace? Escribe, anda* (*mādhā yafᶜalu? yaktubu, yamshī*).

Lexical and morphological considerations are not an impediment to the logical equation of languages. The syntax, however, as seen in the comparison of the above simple phrases—"What does he do?" *Mādhā yafᶜalu?*—puts such an equation in jeopardy. Syntax, which is the structure of complex, integrating linguistic logic, quite naturally varies more from language to language. But syntax, in the final analysis, is the reflection of thought-patterns which from thought-discoveries developed into thought-habits and then turned into thought-rules. We usually operate with thought-rules. Our new, individual thought-discoveries rarely are permitted to develop into common thought-habits, and thus vanish as sporadic phenomena without constituting new rules. But this is not a rigid situation. There are fluctuations in languages, gradual changes, developments. Local colloquialisms become generalized; idiomatic expressions turn from casuistic into analogically formative phenomena; linguistic patterns cross borders and become assimilated by neighboring languages.

It is this latter form of change which concerns us here. Modern Arabic is coming into being only inasmuch as it changes and thus becomes different from nonmodern Arabic—the classical *al-fuṣḥā*. But what does modern Arabic become? The answer that it becomes *itself* is only rhetorically satisfactory. The essence of complex things is always elusive; therefore let us circumscribe the essence in question by wider circles. Modern Arabic has become a usable, functional language. It has done away with things which are not in our present realm of thought and experience and substituted relevant ones for them. Modern Arabic, as the simplistic claim goes, has become simplified; it is grammatically more logical according to one claim and grammatically more flexible and lenient (and thus less disciplined, discipline being a kind of logic) according to another; it has bridged the gap between the classical and the colloquial; and so forth, in ever-widening circles.

All these circumstantial definitions, however, presuppose that the classical language is the opposite of the modern language or at least tends towards its opposite. Such a light upon classical Arabic is time-refracted and therefore not absolutely just. At some historical moment classical Arabic must have been all the things that we should like to see in the modern language. It is equally false to look exclusively for formal differences between the old and the new languages. References to different civilizational environments—those of present relevance and irrelevance—have truth in them, but not all the truth. In the example of the nineteenth-century Arab writers we may see the intimation of a new relevance, but its full comprehension was not possible at that time. Pioneer Arab modernists were seeing the West and modernity with eyes unaided by a linguistic frame of reference. Their helplessness was not due only to a lack of vocabulary, to not being able to call the new things by their right names.

It is here where so many writers blunder. They think that given the words, the nomenclature, comprehension is achieved and subsequent communication of new knowledge is possible. Yet al-Ṭahṭāwī's visit to Europe was like a child's visit to a vast museum of natural science. What remains after such an experience is an impression of a mythical world suspended in mid-air. Scientific tracts of his time read like reports on obscure archaeological excavations. Much of the nomenclature may already be there, but the whole does not fit into a new vision of the world and its objects. This only proves that we do not think in terms of objects but in terms of their correlation and relation to us. For more than one hundred years Arab modernists—both in letters and the sciences—were captivated by the new objects. They saw the trees without realizing that they were in the midst of a forest. They were making a new vocabulary without yet achieving a modern idiom. They did not think like modern men yet, because thought, for all practical purposes, is inseparable from language. The early modernists were neoclassicists, however. They believed in engrafting new words upon the rigid classical linguistic forms. They failed to realize that, culturally, new words bring with them new linguistic contexts which must replace the old ones, and that these new contexts create a new language. Modern Arabic, therefore, is modern only insofar as it is a culturally new language.

Modern Arabic culture, however, is, to an extent difficult to tell, not an autochthonous phenomenon. It is very much something borrowed and assimilated. The bearing of this fact upon the language is not marginal—it is essential. Timidly at first, and massively during the last fifty years, Arabs were understanding the world and their new cultural aspirations through concepts and thought-contexts which could not have been of their making. Western influence was making itself felt not only in vocabulary but also in a new style and rhythm of thought, and thus in a wholly new feeling for the language. A series of assimilated thoughts had to produce a linguistic thought-configuration which had its origin in the influencing culture. An Arab writer trying to come to terms with Anatole France, for example, would find that knowing French to perfection would not suffice, and that knowing classical Arabic equally well was not enough either.

The discovery that there was a mysterious link missing for a successful thought transfusion from the Western into the Arabic culture became a source of frustration, particularly for the literary generation active in the first quarter of the present century, as it was fully committed to innovation. At the same time, it was this generation which put modern Arabic on its present course, which unknowingly defined modern Arabic, and which produced the first firmly rooted and consequential cultural communication with modernity. What enabled all this to happen was the gradual appearance of affinities between Arabic and the modern European family of languages.

Touching upon the subject of supragenealogical linguistic affinities, Hans Wehr discusses E. Schwyzer's concept of cultural linguistic community.[1] The generic category of Western languages—a term we so often use without full conceptual precision—is first of all a cultural phenomenon. Out of a cultural community arises a linguistic community, producing a common linguistic spirit which pervades languages participating in a collective culture and is the expression of linguistic unity beyond genealogical frontiers and differences. Europe has achieved such a far reaching *kulturelle Sprachverwandtschaft* through centuries of internal cultural commerce. Present European thought habits and thought patterns reveal a striking unity of linguistic spirit. The differences of grammatical structure within the European community of languages did not prevent the appearance of lexical-contextual and idiomatic

1. Wehr, "Entwicklung und traditionelle Pflege," pp. 28–29.

cross-borrowings which modulated even individual language structures. The generic concept of Western languages, as an influencing factor upon Arabic, is therefore not a vague, undisciplined generalization but a linguistic and cultural reality.

Another term which has to be defined, if only in the context of our present discussion, is that of "modern languages." On the one hand it is self-evident that contemporary languages are modern. But this is true in a chronological sense only, for in the cultural picture which concerns us here, we understand by "modern languages" only those that are culture-bearing or culture-aspiring in the modern sense. It is the relationship of an individual language to the idea of modern culture, therefore, which determines its modernity. This culture-determined modernity of contemporary languages is thus a measurable entity, and, as a result, we may speak, in a case like that of Arabic, of the language's premodern state, of its classical and then modern orientation, and finally of its approaching the requirements of modernity.

After these definitions we should understand the far-reaching significance of our term—modern Arabic. Through its new lexicon, the thought-shaping context of that lexicon, and last but not least through the great wealth and variety of assimilated idiomatic patterns and literally taken-over phraseological units, the contemporary Arabic literary language has crossed its genealogical linguistic borders and has entered into cultural linguistic affinity with the broad supragenealogical family of modern Western languages. The process of its integration into the Western *Sprachgeist* has of course only begun, but its orientation now seems firm and its pace decidedly fast. Arabic continues, morphologically, to be a Semitic language, still very much the classical *al-fuṣḥā*, but to remain with that definition would be a mistake. The configuration of its syntax now conforms to new, largely non-Semitic thought-dynamics. The modern Arabic mind is becoming an offshoot of the modern Western mind and is retaining fewer and fewer of the rigidly Semitic thought-habits and thus fewer of the classical idiomatic molds and structural particularities. A common modern cultural linguistic spirit is becoming the defining factor of modern Arabic.

We may now assert that as a culture-bearing language modern Arabic is not and shall not be a "simplified" language. This idea clearly belongs to the perplexed generation of the first quarter of the present century. As for the language becoming grammatically more logical, such a claim is entirely relative. The classical language was "more" logical in its own cultural context. The modern language has to be equally logical in its own time and culture. The classical Arabic style of thought duly reflected the classical Arabic civilization. The modern style has different purposes to fulfill.

Then, too, modern Arabic can only be viewed as more flexible than its classical parent with reference to a new dimension of expression—literary expression, mostly—for which it serves as a tool. The limitations of the classical Arabic written language were the result of the restricted formal scope of Arabic literary genres and other written manifestations. The insufficient recognition prose genres received as means of higher literary expression produced a concentration on a formalistic poetic use of the language. This alienated the language from the dynamism of live speech. The formal conventions of narrative literature became congealed in the *maqāmāt.* The stylistic combination of functional scholarly formalism with anecdotic departures, which characterizes medieval Arabic historical and biographical literature, did not provide for a full exploitation of the expressive possibilities of the language. In a particular way this formal rigidity affected the development of dialogue. We do not know how the ninth- or tenth-century Arabs spoke or would have spoken. Writers like al-Jāḥiẓ give us scanty hints, but those hints only serve to confirm the suspicion that there must have been much more to the expressive range of the classical language than what is recorded. The lack of a classical Arabic theatre is, of course, most regrettable in this respect.

What older Arabic literature thus tells us, linguistically,

is that there existed rather strict and narrow boundaries within which linguistic thought-expression could move, and that the structural rigidity of Arabic grammar was not the only determining factor of the development, or lack of development, of the Arabic language. The general cultural framework was actually the real determinant of the language. Whatever complexities that language possessed were formally grammatical only in a secondary degree. First of all they were the modes in which the medieval Arabic mind worked. They were thus an aspect of that mind. The modern Arab mind is acquiring its own complexities which must be met by the language in such a form as to render them transparent. And here, too, grammar ought not to be considered as a measure of complexity or logic.

As for defining modern Arabic by its capacity and function to bridge the gap between the classical and the colloquial languages, this is hardly a sound linguistic approach to the solution of the problem of diglossia. Theorizing in this direction is based on mistaken premises to begin with. It assumes that the modern language will be a compromise between those two extremes, and that the two extremes constitute the ideal on one hand and a degeneration on the other. Modern Arabic would thus be something in between —neither quite good nor entirely bad. Such an assumption rests on a double fallacy, since a language's function is expressive and not cultural-ideological in the historical sense, and since the assumption does not take into account the possibility that modern Arabic might take an entirely different line of development.

As already proposed above, it is precisely this latter possibility—a third road—which is bound to become the true line of development of the Arabic language. Modern Arabic is moving away from both the classical and the colloquial languages. While retaining the morphological structure of classical Arabic, syntactically and, above all, stylistically it is coming ever closer to the form and spirit of the large, suprageneological family of Western culture-bearing languages. Provided modern Arabic remains in that sphere, it may take no more than two or three generations for it to become a highly integrated member of the Western cultural linguistic family, sharing fully in a common modern linguistic spirit. The Arabic syntax will then have undergone far-reaching changes dictated by modern thought-dynamics. The categories of the verbal and the nominal sentences will not be the main syntactical characteristics. Instead, the notion of meaning-stress will dictate the order of sentence elements. This will suppose a healthy shift in attitude from the formalistic grammatical one to a dynamic, stylistic one. The Arabic sentence will also become richer in subordinate clauses, and their order and coordination will be as flexible as modern thought-habits. A clear trend away from syntactical simplicity can already be observed. Style models like those provided by Ṭaha Ḥusayn and his generation are too uninvolved and bare to be of much use to even present-day writers and poets. The trend towards a new complexity, however, can not lead backwards to classical models. New models from the external sources of cultural and linguistic contact will take their place.

There can be little fear that these now apparent trends might be interrupted or drastically diverted. Linguistic processes, once started, are capable of self-perpetuation from within the language. In fact, secondary developments, which will be the results of primary idiomatic borrowings, will naturally and effortlessly produce the main stock of modern expressions or molds of expression. Analogical imitation of borrowed expressions will entail chains of effective stylistic derivations which will sound authentic within the new spirit of the language. The future of the Arabic language will thus not lie in artificial compromises between the two native linguistic sources of classicism and colloquialism, which work against each other, but rather in a straight line of development out of a classical Semitic morphology towards a new, largely non-Semitic syntax which will be dictated by habits of thought rather than by habits of live speech. Only then, in possession of a language by which to think, will the Arabs be able to overcome the problem of conflicting colloquialism and classicism. The traditional *al-fuṣḥā* was and is helpless against the colloquial languages because it does not reflect the thought habits of its users. The modern Arabic language which we try to define and project here will become a language for modern, fully developed thought; as such it will have the vitality to replace the spoken dialects without artificially suppressing them.

Bibliography

ᶜAbbās, ᵓIḥsān, and Najm, Muḥammad Yūsuf. *Al-Shiᶜr al-ᶜArabī fī al-Mahjar*. Beirut: 1957.

ᶜAbbūd, Mārūn. *ᶜAlā al-Miḥakk. Naẓarāt wa ᵓĀrāᵓ fī al-Shiᶜr wa al-Shuᶜarāᵓ*. Beirut: 1946.

———. *Judud wa Quḍamāᵓ*. Beirut: 1954.

ᶜAbd al-Lāh, Muḥammad ᶜAbd al-Ḥalīm. *Shams al-Kharīf*. Cairo: 1953.

ᵓAdab. Vol. 2, no. 1 (Winter 1963).

ᶜAlī, Muṣṭafā. *Maḥaḍarāt ᶜan Maᶜrūf al-Ruṣāfī*. Cairo: 1954.

al-ᵓĀlūsī, Maḥmūd Shukrī. *Bulūgh al-ᵓArab fī Maᶜrifat ᵓAḥwāl al-ᶜArab*. 2nd ed. 3 vols. Cairo, A.H. 1342.

ᵓAmīn, ᵓAḥmad. *Ḍuḥā al-ᵓIslām*. 5th ed. 3 vols. Cairo: 1956.

———. *Fajr al-ᵓIslām*. 7th ed. Cairo: 1955.

———. "Mustaqbal al-ᵓAdab al-ᶜArabī." *Al-Thaqāfah*, year 6 (1944), no. 280.

———. *Ẓuhr al-ᵓIslām*. 2d ed. 4 vols. Cairo: 1957.

ᵓAnīs, ᵓIbrāhīm, *Dalālat al-ᵓAlfāẓ*. 2d ed. Cairo: 1963.

Apollo. Vols. 1–2 Cairo: September 1932–May 1934.

al-ᶜAqqād, ᶜAbbās Maḥmūd, "Ḥarb al-Lughah." *Al-Kitāb*. Vol. 11, year 7, no. 5 (May 1952), pp. 536–40.

Badr, ᶜAbd al-Muḥsin Ṭaha. *Taṭawwur al-Riwāyah al-ᶜArabīyah al-Ḥadīthah fī Miṣr (1870–1938)*. Cairo: 1963.

Bloomfield, Leonard. *Language*. New York: 1938.

Bocthor, Ellious. *Dictionnaire français-arabe*. Revised and supplemented by Caussin de Perceval. Paris: 1848.

al-Bustānī, Buṭrus. *Muḥīṭ al-Muḥīṭ*. Vol. 1. Beirut: 1867.
al-Bustānī, Fuʾad ʾIfrām. *Al-Shaykh ʾIbrāhīm al-Yāzijī: Fī al-Lughah wa al-ʾAdab*. Beirut: 1952.
al-Bustānī, Sulaymān. *ʾIlyādhat Hūmīrus*. Cairo: 1904.
Cachia, Pierre. *Taha Husayn, His Place in the Egyptian Literary Renaissance*. London: Luzac and Co., 1956.
Dozy, Reinhart P. A., *Supplement aux dictionnaires arabes*. 2 vols. Leiden: Brill, 1881.
al-Dusūqī, ᶜUmar. *Fī al-ʾAdab al-Ḥadīth*. 3d ed. Cairo: 1954.
The Encyclopaedia of Islam. Leiden–London: 1936.
Fahmī, Ḥasan Ḥusayn. *Al-Marjiᶜ fī Taᶜrīb al-Muṣṭalaḥāt al-ᶜIlmīyah wa al-Fannīyah wa al-Handasīyah*. Cairo: 1958.
Fleisch, Henri. *Al-ᶜArabīyah al-Fuṣḥā: Naḥwa Binaʾin Lughawīyin Jadīdin*. Translated by ᶜAbd al-Ṣabūr Shāhīn. Beirut: 1966.
———. *Traité de philologie arabe*. Vol. 1. Beirut: 1961.
Furayḥah, ʾAnīs, *Al-Lahajāt wa ʾUslūb Dirāsatihā*. Cairo: 1955.
———. *Naḥwa ᶜArabīyatin Muyassarah*. Beirut: 1955.
al-Futayyiḥ, ʾAḥmad. *Taʾrīkh al-Majmaᶜ al-ᶜIlmī al-ᶜArabī*. Damascus: 1956.
Ghuṣn, al-Khūrī Mārūn. *Ḥayāt al-Lughah wa Mawtuhā. Al-Lughah al-ᶜĀmmīyah*. Beirut: 1925.
al-Ḥakīm, Tawfīq. *Fann al-ʾAdab*. Cairo: 1952.
———. Vol. 2. *Qiṣaṣ Tawfīq al-Ḥakīm*. Cairo: 1949.
Hammūdah, ᶜAbd al-Wahhāb. *Al-Tajdīd fī al-ʾAdab al-Miṣrī al-Ḥadīth*, Cairo: n.d.
al-Ḥarīrī, ʾAbū Muḥammad al-Qāsim Ibn ᶜAlī. *Kitāb Durrat al-Ghawwāṣ fī ʾAwhām al-Khawāṣṣ*. Edited by Heinrich Thorbecke. Leipzig: 1871.
Ḥasan, ᶜAbbās. *Al-Lughah wa al-Naḥw bayna al-Qadīm wa al-Ḥadīth*. Cairo: 1966.
Ḥasanayn, Fuʾād. "Al-Dakhīl fī al-Lughah al-ᶜArabīyah." *Majallat Kullīyat al-ʾĀdāb*. Vol. 10, pt. 2 (December 1948), pp. 75–112; vol. 11, pt. 1 (May 1949), pp. 25–56; vol. 11, pt. 2 (December 1949), pp. 1–36; vol. 12, pt. 1 (May 1950), pp. 37–74.
Haykal, Muḥammad Ḥusayn. *Zaynab. Manāẓir wa ʾAkhlāq Rīfīyah*. 1st ed. (1914) Cairo: 1963.
Ḥiwār. Vol. 3, no. 3 (Beirut: March–April 1965).
Ḥusayn, Ṭaha. *Ḥadīth al-ʾArbaᶜāʾ*. Vol. 3. Cairo: 1957.
———. *Maᶜa al-Mutanabbī*. Cairo: 1957.
———. *Min ʾAdabinā al-Muᶜāṣir*. 2d ed. Cairo: 1959.
al-Ḥuṣrī, Sāṭiᶜ. *ʾĀrāʾ wa ʾAḥādīth fī al-Lughah wa al-ʾAdab*. Beirut: 1958.
Ibn ᶜArabī. *Tarjumān al-Ashwāq*. Beirut: 1961.
Ibn al-Athīr, Ḍiyāʾ al-Dīn. *Al-Jāmiᶜ al-Kabīr fī Ṣināᶜat al-Mawzūn min al-Kalām wa al-Manthūr*. Baghdad: 1956.

Ibn al-Fāriḍ. *Dīwān*. Beirut: 1962.
Ibn Fāris, ᵓAḥmad. *Al-Ṣāḥibī fī Fiqh al-Lughah wa Sunan al-ᶜArab fī Kalāmihā*. Cairo: 1910.
Ibn Jinnī, ᵓAbū al-Fatḥ ᶜUthmān. *Al-Khaṣāᵓiṣ*. Vols. 1–3. Cairo: 1952, 1955, 1956.
Ibn Khaldūn. *Al-Muqaddimah*. See: Quatremère and Rosenthal.
Ibn al-Muᶜtazz, ᶜAbd al-Lāh. *Kitāb al-Badīᶜ*. London: 1935.
Ibn Shuhayd. *Risālat al-Tawābiᶜ wa al-Zawābiᶜ*. Beirut: 1951.
ᵓIdrīs, Yūsuf. *Lughat al-ᵓĀy-ᵓāy*. Cairo: 1965.
ᶜInān, ᶜAbd al-Lāh. *Dawlat al-ᵓIslām fī al-ᵓAndalus. Al-ᶜAṣr al-ᵓAwwal*. Cairo: 1960.
al-Jāḥiẓ. *Al-Bayān wa al-Tabyīn*. Cairo: 1960.
———. *Al-Bukhalāᵓ*. Cairo: 1958.
———. *Rasāᵓil al-Jāḥiẓ*. Vol. 1. Cairo: 1964.
Jawād, Muṣṭafā. "Wasāᵓil al-Nuhūḍ bi al-Lughah al-ᶜArabīyah." *Al-ᵓUstādh*. Vols. 7–8. Baghdad: 1959–60.
[Jubrān, Jubrān Khalīl]. *Jubrān Khalīl Jubrān: Al-Majmūᶜah al-Kāmilah li Muᵓallafātihi*. Beirut: 1959.
Junblāt, Kamāl. *Fī Majrā al-Siyāsah al-Lubnānīyah: ᵓAwḍāᶜ wa Takhṭīṭ*. Beirut: 1959.
al-Jundī, ᵓAnwar. *Al-Lughah al-ᶜArabīyah bayna Ḥumātihā wa Khuṣūmiha*. Cairo: n.d.
———. *Nazaᶜāt al-Tajdīd fī al-ᵓAdab al-ᶜArabī al-Muᶜāṣir: Min Thawrat 1919 ᵓilā Thawrat 1952*. Cairo: 1957.
al-Jurjāni, (al-Qāḍi) ᶜAlī ᶜAbd al-ᶜAzīz. *Al-Wasāṭah bayna al-Mutanabbī wa Khuṣūmihi*. 4th ed. Cairo: 1966.
Kāmil, Murād. *Dalālāt al-ᵓAlfāẓ al-ᶜArabīyah wa Taṭawwuruhā*. Cairo: 1963.
Khafājī, Muḥammad ᶜAbd al-Munᶜim. *Al-Shiᶜr wa al-Tajdīd*. Cairo: n.d.
al-Khūlī, ᵓAmīn. *Manāhij Tajdīd fī al-Naḥw wa al-Balāghah wa al-Tafsīr wa al-ᵓAdab*. Cairo: 1961.
al-Khūlī, ᵓAmīn. *Fann al-Qawl*. Cairo: 1947.
al-Kirmalī, ᵓAnastās Mārī. *Nushūᵓ al-Lughah al-ᶜArabīyah wa Iktihāluhā*. Cairo: 1938.
Lane, Edward William. *Arabic-English Lexicon*. New York: Frederick Ungar, 1955.
Al-Lisān al-ᶜArabī. Nos. 1–4. Rabat: 1964–66.
Lughat al-ᶜArab. Founded and edited by Anastase-Marie de Saint-Elie (al-Kirmalī). Baghdad.
Luṭfī al-Sayyid, ᵓAḥmad. *Al-Muntakhabāt*. 2 vols. Cairo: 1945.
al-Maᶜarrī, ᵓAbū al-ᶜAlāᵓ. *Risālat al-Ghufrān*. Cairo: 1950.
al-Maghribī, ᶜAbd al-Qādir. *Kitāb al-Ishtiqāq wa al-Taᶜrīb*. 2d ed. Cairo: 1947.
Maḥfūẓ, Najīb. *Bayna al-Qaṣrayn*. Cairo: 1956.
———. *Bidāyah wa Nihāyah*. Cairo: 1958.
———. *Mīrāmār*. Cairo: 1967.
———. *Al-Qāhirah al-Jadīdah*. Cairo: 1958.

Maḥfūẓ, Najīb. *Qaṣr al-Shawq*. Cairo: 1957.
———. *Al-Sarāb*. Cairo: 1948.
———. *Al-Sukkarīyah*. Cairo: 1958.
———. *Al-Ṭarīq*. Cairo: 1964.
———. *Zuqāq al-Midaqq*. 2d. ed. Cairo: 1955.
Mainz, Ernst. *Zur Grammatik des modernen Schriftarabisch*. Hamburg: 1931.
Majallat al-Majmaᶜ al-ᶜIlmī al-ᶜArabī. Damascus: 1921–.
Majallat Majmaᶜ al-Lughah al-ᶜArabīyah al-Malakī. Cairo: 1935–.
Majmaᶜ al-Lughah al-ᶜArabīyah al-Malakī. Maḥāḍir al-Jalasāt. Cairo: 1936.
Majmaᶜ Fuᵓād al-ᵓAwwal li al-Lughah al-ᶜArabīyah: Muᵓtamar al-Majmaᶜ—Sanah 1944. Taysīr al-Kitābah al-ᶜArabīyah. Cairo: 1946.
Majmūᶜat al-Buḥūth wa al-Muḥāḍarāt—Majmaᶜ al-Lughah al-ᶜArabīyah. Vols. 1–3. Cairo: 1960–62–.
al-Makhzūmī, Mahdī. *Fī al-Naḥw al-ᶜArabī: Naqd wa Tawjīh*. Sidon-Beirut: 1964.
Malāᵓikah, Nāzik. ᶜĀshiqat al-Layl. 2d. ed. Beirut: 1960.
Mandūr, Muḥammad. *Fī al-Mīzān al-Jadīd*. Cairo: 1944.
———. *Al-Naqd al-Manhajī ᶜinda al-ᶜArab*. Cairo: 1948.
———. *Al-Shiᶜr al-Miṣrī Baᶜda Shawqī*. Cairo: 1955.
al-Maqdisī, ᵓAnīs al-Khūrī. *Al-Ittijāhāt al-ᵓAdabīyah fī al-ᶜĀlam al-ᶜArabī al-Ḥadīth*. 2d ed. Beirut: 1960.
———. *Taṭawwur al-ᵓAsālīb al-Nathrīyah fī al-ᵓAdab al-ᶜArabī*. Vol. 1. Beirut: 1935.
Maẓhar, ᵓIsmāᶜīl. "Al-Lughah al-ᶜArabīyah wa Ḥājatuhā ᵓilā Muᶜjamin Lughawīyin Taᵓrīkhīyin." *Al-Majallah*. Year 4, no. 4 (April 1960), pp. 21–22.
Maẓhar, ᵓIsmāᶜīl. *Tajdīd al-ᶜArabīyah*. Cairo: n.d.
al-Māzinī, ᵓIbrāhīm ᶜAbd al-Qadir. *Ḥiṣād al-Hashīm*. 2d ed. Cairo: 1932.
Minutes. See under *Majmaᶜ al-Lughah al-ᶜArabīyah al-Malakī*.
Monteil, Vincent. *L'arabe moderne*. Paris: C. Klincksieck, 1960.
Murūwah, ᵓAdīb. *Al-Ṣiḥāfah al-ᶜArabīyah: Nashᵓatuhā wa Taṭawwuruhā*. Beirut: 1961.
Murūwah, Ḥusayn. *Qaḍāyā ᵓAdabīyah*. Cairo: 1956.
Mūsā, Salāmah. *Al-ᵓAdab li al-Shaᶜb*. Cairo: 1956.
Muṣṭafā, ᵓIbrāhīm. *ᵓIḥyāᵓ al-Naḥw*. Cairo: 1937.
al-Mutanabbī, ᵓAbū Ṭayyib. *Dīwān*. Vol. 1. Commentary by Nāṣīf al-Yāzijī. Beirut: 1964.
Naqqāsh, Mārūn. *ᵓArzat Lubnān*. Beirut: 1869.
Nadīm, ᶜAbd al-Lāh. *Al-Ishtiqāq*. Cairo: 1956.
The Nakāᵓid of Jarīr and al-Farazdak. Edited by Anthony Ashley Bevan. Vol. 1. Leiden: Brill, 1905.
Nakhlah, ᵓAmīn. *Al-Ḥarakah al-Lughawīyah fī Lubnān fī al-Ṣadr al-ᵓAwwal min al-Qarn al-ᶜIshrīn*. 2d ed. Beirut: 1958.

Nuᶜaymah, Mīkhāᵓīl, and others. *Fī al-ᵓAdab al-Ḥadīth*. Beirut: American University of Beirut, 1954.
Nuᶜaymah, Mīkhāᵓīl. *Al-Ghirbāl*. Cairo: 1957.
Quatremère, E., ed. "Prolegomènes d'Ebn-Khaldoun." *Notices et Extraits des manuscrits de la Bibliothèque Impériale*. Vol. 8. Paris: Académie des Inscriptions et Belles-Lettres. 1958.
al-Rāfiᶜī, Muṣṭafā Ṣādiq. *Taᵓrīkh ᵓĀdāb al-ᶜArab*. Vol. 3. 3d ed. Cairo: 1954.
Reckendorf, H. *Arabische Syntax*. Heidelberg: 1921.
Revista del Instituto de Estudios Islámicos en Madrid. Vols. 7–8. Madrid: 1959–60, pp. 437–95.
Riḍā, Muḥyī al-Dīn, ed. *Balāghat al-ᶜArab fī al-Qarn al-ᶜIshrīn*. 2d ed. Cairo: 1924.
Rosenthal, Franz, tr. *Ibn Khaldūn. The Muqaddima. An Introduction to History*. Vol. 3. New York: Pantheon Books, 1958.
Saᶜīd, Naffūsah Zakariyā. *Taᵓrīkh al-Daᶜwah ᵓilā al-ᶜĀmmīyah wa ᵓĀthāruhā fī Miṣr*. Alexandria: 1964.
al-Sāmarrāᵓī, ᶜĀmir Rashīd. *ᵓĀrāᵓ fī al-ᶜArabīyah*. Baghdad: 1965.
al-Sāmarrāᵓī, ᵓIbrāhīm. *Lughat al-Shiᶜr Bayna Jīlayn*. Beirut: 1965.
———. *Al-Taṭawwur al-Lughawī al-Taᵓrīkhī*. Cairo: 1966.
Ṣarrūf, Fuᵓād. "Siyar ᵓAlfāẓ ᶜArabīyah Mustaḥdathah." *Al-ᵓAbḥāth*. Vol. 16, no. 3 (September 1963), pp. 281–98.
al-Shābbī, ᵓAbū al-Qāsim. *ᵓAghānī al-Ḥayāh*. Cairo: 1955.
al-Sharīf, Ḥasan. "Tabsīṭ Qawāᶜid al-ᶜArabīyah." *Al-Hilāl* (August 1938), pp. 1108–19.
Sheikho, Louis [Shaykhū, Lūyis]. *Al-ᵓĀdāb al-ᶜArabīyah fī al-Rubᶜ al-ᵓAwwal min al-Qarn al-ᶜIshrīn*. Beirut: 1926.
al-Shayyāl, Jamāl al-Dīn. *Taᵓrīkh al-Tarjamah wa al-Ḥarakah al-Thaqāfīyah fī ᶜAṣr Muḥammad ᶜAlī*. Cairo: 1951.
al-Shidyāq, ᵓAḥmad Fāris. *Sirr al-Liyāl fī al-Qalb wa al-ᵓIbdāl*. Istanbul: 1867 (A.H. 1284).
al-Shihābī, Muṣṭafā. "Khawāṭir fī al-Qawmīyah al-ᶜArabīyah wa al-Lughah al-Fuṣḥā." *Majallat Majmaᶜ al-Lughah al-ᶜArabiyah bi Dimashq*. Vol. 36, pt. 3 (July 1961).
Sībawayh, ᶜAmr Ibn ᶜUthmān. *Kitāb Sībawayh*. 2 vols. Berlin: 1895–1900.
Shiᶜr. Vol. 6, no. 22 (Spring 1962), p. 110.
Siddiqi, Abdussatar. *Studien über die persischen Fremdwörter im klassischen Arabisch*. Göttingen: 1919.
Sulaymān, Mūsā. *Al-ᵓAdab al-Qaṣaṣī ᶜinda al-ᶜArab*. Beirut: 1956.
al-Suyūṭī. *Al-ᵓItqān*. 3d ed. Cairo: 1951.
al-Ṭahṭāwī, Rifāᶜah. *Takhlīs al-ᵓIbrīz fī Talkhīṣ Bārīz*. Cairo: n.d.
Taymūr, ᵓAḥmad. *Al-Samāᶜ wa al-Qiyās*. Cairo: 1955.
Taymūr, Maḥmud. *Mushkilāt al-Lughah al-ᶜArabīyah*. Cairo: 1956.

al-ʿUrayyiḍ, ʾIbrāhīm. *Min al-Shiʿr al-Ḥadīth*. Beirut: 1958.
Al-ʾUsbūʿ al-ʿArabī. No. 382 (March 10, 1966), p. 47.
Wehr, Hans. *A Dictionary of Modern Written Arabic*. Ithaca, N.Y.: Cornell University Press, 1961.
———. *Die Besonderheiten des heutigen Hocharabischen mit Berücksichtigung der Einwirkung der Europäischen Sprachen*. Berlin: 1934.
———. "Entwicklung und traditionelle Pflege der arabischen Schriftsprache in der Gegenwart." *Zeitung der Deutschen Morgenländischen Gesellschaft*. Vol. 97 (1943), pp. 16–46.
Wright, W. *A Grammar of the Arabic Language*. 3d ed. 2 vols. Cambridge: Cambridge University Press, 1955.
Yāqūt, [ʾAbū ʿAbd al-Lāh]. *Muʿjam al-ʾUdabāʾ*. Vol. 12 (20 vols.), Cairo: 1936.
al-Yāzijī, ʾIbrāhīm. *Lughat al-Jarāʾid*. Cairo: 1901.
al-Zaḥlāwī, Ḥabīb. *ʾUdabāʾ Muʿāṣirūn*. Cairo: 1935.
Zaydān, Jurjī. *ʾAsīr al-Mutamahdī*. 4th ed. Cairo: 1924.
———. *Al-Falsafah al-Lughawīyah wa al-ʾAlfāẓ al-ʿArabīyah*. Revised by Murād Kāmil. Cairo: n.d.
———. *Al-Lughah al-ʿArabīyah Kāʾin Ḥayy*. Revised by Murād Kāmil. Cairo: n.d.

Index